Christianity and World Religions

ADAM HAMILTON

Christianity AND World Religions

Wrestling With Questions People Ask

ABINGDON PRESS

NASHVILLE

Christianity and World Religions:
Wrestling With Questions People Ask

Copyright © 2005 by Abingdon Press.

Scripture quotations in this publication, unless otherwise indicated, are from the New Revised Standard Version of the Bible, copyrighted © 1989 by the Division of Christian Education of the National Council of the Churches of Christ in the United States of America, and are used by permission.

This book is printed on acid-free, elemental chlorine-free paper.

ISBN 0-687-49490-7
ISBN 0-687-49430-3

05 06 07 08 09 10 11 12 13 14—10 9 8 7 6 5 4 3 2 1
MANUFACTURED IN THE UNITED STATES OF AMERICA

To my father, Mark Hamilton,
who has spent much of his life living and working
among people of other faiths.

ACKNOWLEDGMENTS

This book would not have been possible in its present form were it not for the people of the United Methodist Church of the Resurrection and their love for learning and being stretched to think about important but challenging topics. They graciously allow me the time to research and prepare sermons such as the ones on which this book was based.

Nor would this book have been possible without the help of my assistant, Sue Thompson, who tirelessly serves Christ and without whose help I could never preach, teach, or write.

I must acknowledge the staff of the Church of the Resurrection, all of whom are remarkable. I would lift up the particular contributions of our worship team and the members of the Saving Grace Productions team, who made possible the interviews I conducted with leaders of the other major religions. Among the staff who make it possible for me to devote the time and effort to develop a resource such as this is Steve Eginoire, whose ministry in our church has had a significant impact on my life and whose friendship and support in the face of the criticism that comes from preaching and writing on this kind of topic have been a source of strength and blessing to me.

Finally, I want to acknowledge the role my wife, LaVon, and my daughters, Danielle and Rebecca, play in my life. Their love, encouragement, and ideas continue to shape my life in so many ways.

CONTENTS

CHAPTER 1

Questions People Ask

In the time of King Herod, after Jesus was born in Bethlehem of Judea, wise men from the East came to Jerusalem, asking, "Where is the child who has been born king of the Jews? For we observed his star at its rising, and have come to pay him homage."...There, ahead of them, went the star that they had seen at its rising, until it stopped over the place where the child was. When they saw that the star had stopped, they were overwhelmed with joy. On entering the house, they saw the child with Mary his mother; and they knelt down and paid him homage. Then, opening their treasure chests, they offered him gifts of gold, frankincense, and myrrh.

(Matthew 2:1-2, 9b-11)

At some point in our lives, each of us will be confronted with the claims of persons of other faiths—coworkers, neighbors, friends. Our children will study other faiths in school, have friends who are of other religions, and live in a world that is increasingly diverse.

We live in a world that is very different from the one in which most of us grew up. Many of us went to school without having a single Buddhist, Muslim, or Hindu classmate. Some

Americans grew up never knowing any Jewish families because there were no synagogues in the small towns in which they lived. It is not that way anymore. Our society is more religiously diverse than ever. Yet many Americans know very little about Hinduism, Buddhism, Islam, and even Judaism. But the likelihood today is that one of your neighbors, one of your coworkers, or one of your children's teachers at school is a person of another faith.

In addition, our world is divided and even at war along religious lines. Muslims are in conflict with Christians. At the time of this writing, in the territory that separates India from Pakistan, Hindus and Muslims are engaged in a conflict that has nearly resulted in nuclear war. In the tinderbox we call the Holy Land, Muslims and Jews continue to engage in armed struggle for land both claim as their own.

In light of these facts of modern life, it is essential that Christians seek to understand the faiths of others—to know how these faiths are similar to and different from their own faith—and to use that understanding to build bridges with others so that we might grow in our faith, seek peace in our world, love our neighbor, and find positive ways to share the gospel.

Jesus Christ told his followers to go into the world and make disciples (Matthew 28:16-20). How can we as Christians do that effectively with persons of other faiths if we have no idea what they believe? How can we share Christ in a sensitive way if we have no idea what someone else's idea of truth is?

In this book we will be examining Christianity and four of the other major world religions. If we are honest, the thought of contemplating the claims of other religions makes most of us a bit nervous. It is threatening to our own faith. What if the other religions are right? Many of us are Christians, frankly, because our parents were Christians. We did not necessarily choose Christianity; it chose us. So, when faced with the claims of another religion, we feel some uncertainty. Can my faith withstand a serious consideration of another's religion? What if my picture of God is wrong? What if I cannot demonstrate the ultimate truthfulness of the gospel? As a pastor, I feel the weight of these questions. I do not want to do anything to undermine your faith; my hope is to help you *grow* in faith. Yet I believe that if Christianity does offer us the truth about God, it can withstand a serious study of other religions. If it is not ultimately true, then our task should be to discern what is true and pursue this truth.

I approach this study as a Christian. I recognize that I cannot be completely objective, no matter how hard I might attempt to be. I approach my own study of the world religions with an effort at being open and understanding, and with a willingness to see truth wherever it may be found. But my starting point, and the lens through which I see the world, is my own faith in Jesus Christ and my Christian experience.

Studying some of the major world religions raises a host of questions that we will wrestle with throughout this book. In this first chapter, we will focus on four key questions:

(1) Why are there so many different religions?

(2) How should Christians view other religions?

(3) How is God at work in other religions?

(4) What is the fate of those who earnestly pursue God through other religions?

With regard to this last question, I will point toward some conclusions, while inviting you to think carefully about this issue for yourself. I am inclined to be a bit more agnostic on this question than some Christians on either the right or the left; yet I have leanings which I will share, inviting you to push back and formulate your own views in the light of Scripture and the nature and character of God revealed in Jesus Christ.

After considering these initial questions, we will explore four major world religions, one per chapter: Hinduism, Buddhism, Islam, and Judaism. In each chapter I will provide a historical context for the religion; present some of its basic stories, traditions, and beliefs; and describe differences between that religion and Christianity. In the final chapter we will attempt to distill the essence of Christianity, as I understand it.

Before beginning, I will make a disclaimer. In preparation for this book I spent considerable time studying the four religions. I took courses. I carefully read books; websites; and, especially, sacred texts. I visited mosques, temples, and religious centers to ask questions and to attend worship. I had the blessing of interviewing a leading figure of each faith in my own city, whose wisdom I drew upon and whose words, with permission, I have quoted. But I will tell you without hesitation that this preparation in no way qualifies me as an expert.

This study should be seen as a beginning guide to exploring the world religions. I encourage you to conduct some research of your own—reading; studying; and, most of all, talking with people of other faiths. In your conversations with people of other faiths, as you seek to understand and demonstrate respect for their experiences and their teachings, you will likely find your own faith strengthened. In addition, your willingness to listen and learn from people of other faiths may lead them to invite you to share your faith with them as well.

Why Are There So Many Different Religions?

Some people look at the multitude of religions and believe their existence in itself offers proof that there is no God; surely, they reason, God would have made clear the one right path.

The multiplicity of forms of religious expression suggests to these people that God must be a human invention. But I see just the opposite in the varieties of religions. For me, the fact that human beings have had religious thoughts, feelings, yearnings, questions, and experiences throughout every culture, continent, and time points to the reality of God. The fact that all these people, independent of one another, have sensed the same thing, though they may speak of their experience of the divine in different terms, leads me to conclude that there is some reality behind these shared common experiences.

As we survey human history, we find that human beings have always had religious needs, questions, and experiences. Whether you live in Central Africa or Central Europe, when you have a loved one who dies, you long to believe there is something beyond this life. When you see something absolutely magnificent in nature, whether you live in Canada or in Saudi Arabia, something inside you wants to cry out praise to the One who created such beauty. When you spend quiet time alone in prayer, whether you are a Jew in Jerusalem, a Hindu in Calcutta, or a Christian in Kansas City, there is a sense of peace that permeates your heart and mind. And there are times when all of us, regardless of where we live, sense that we have received an insight that came from somewhere beyond ourselves. These are nearly universal experiences, all of which point, I believe, to the ultimate reality of God.

Leaving aside, for a moment, the realm of religion, it is not uncommon for two human beings to have the same experience and give different explanations for it. Sometimes their descriptions of the experience may be similar, but their conclusions regarding the meaning of the experience may be quite different. There *is* an objective reality they both seek to understand, but both are not necessarily correct in their understanding. One or the other may be closer to the truth—or both may have misunderstood the experience. More likely, each of them will be partly right.

After my wife and I go to the movies, we talk about the film as we walk to our car. "Well, what did you think?" I will ask. Sometimes, as I am listening to what she says, I will look at her and wonder, *Did you see the same movie I just saw?* We saw the exact same movie; but she experienced it in one way, and I experienced it in quite another. In a similar way I believe human beings share common religious experiences; but they see them, or understand them, in different ways.

Why should it surprise us that human beings in different places have come up with different solutions to the puzzle of our religious questions, yearnings, and experiences? From a theological point of view, God is so far beyond our human comprehension (The Bible speaks of God's ways as "unsearchable," a term that could be used to describe not only God's ways but also God's very nature.) that all our language about God ultimately fails to describe God adequately. We do not have the logical categories or the mental capability necessary to comprehend all there is to know about God. The apostle Paul captured this point well when he wrote in 1 Corinthians 13:9, 12, "We know only in part.... For now we see in a mirror, dimly." Again, the greatness of God and the smallness of our human minds might lead us to expect that different people will understand their experiences of God in different ways and that we will all be a bit surprised when we actually see God face-to-face!

The question of religious differences partly has to do with how God allows us to learn. I believe that in many ways we learn the same way our children learn. Children are not born with all the information they need in order to be functioning human beings. Instead, they have certain yearnings and

instincts and will spend their whole lives learning and gaining
more information about the world around them. Likewise,
when it comes to human beings understanding the things
of God, we have yearnings, experiences, and intuitions about
God. Then we spend the rest of our lives trying to make sense
of these. (If we are atheists, we devote our energy to explain-
ing them away.) The classic definition of theology is "faith
seeking understanding"—the lifelong task of making sense of
our experiences of God.

Finally, when it comes to the history of religion among
human beings, as a race we are also growing in our understanding of God. The development of religion has progressed
from much more primitive to more sophisticated over time.
Even within the Bible itself we see this development. We find
that Abraham came from a family of polytheists, yet God was
revealed to Abraham in such a way that monotheism took hold
among his descendants. Likewise certain ethical imperatives
were lost on Abraham and the other patriarchs of the Hebrew
faith; but later, in the days of Moses, God revealed and further
clarified his will. God seems to allow the human race to develop
and grow in its understanding of God over time, revealing himself little by little to humanity.

God's way is, in part, to allow human beings to discover
certain things for themselves, learning at times by trial and
error. As a parent, I understand how this works—for example,
with homework. I think particularly of times when my daughter Rebecca asks me to help her with vocabulary assignments.
She starts asking me questions about the meaning of certain
words, and I immediately want to give her all the answers; but
then I realize she will not learn this way. So I try to give her
hints, and I make her look up the words in the dictionary, and
I require her to muddle through. I know that in doing things

this way she will get things wrong at times. Yet this is how she learns. Even if she makes mistakes at times, she learns from the experience.

Over the millennia, this is how God has allowed humanity to learn and grow as a race, not only in the realm of religion, but in the sciences as well. People once thought the earth was the center of the universe. God did not find it important to correct our faulty understandings. Instead, God let us explore new things and finally discover for ourselves that the earth revolves around the sun. I believe that the same may be true of the development of religion. In looking at God's grace and patience in allowing human beings to seek to know him without giving them all the answers, I begin to make sense of the various religions of the world and the history of religion.

About 3,800 years ago, most people on our planet were polytheists. They believed in a multitude of gods. When they felt religious yearnings, they could not fathom that everything could be created and ruled by one being; so they attributed their experiences to different gods and goddesses. God seemed to be patient, waiting for just the right time to reveal the truth that there is but one God. There is no evidence in the Bible that God was angry with Abraham's father, Terah, for failing to be a monotheist. But there came a time when God finally said to humanity, "Now I want to help you." And just as I give hints to my daughter when helping her with her homework, God gave a "hint" to help humanity discover the truth.

Theologians call these hints "special revelation"—ways that God has directly or indirectly sought to guide our inquiry. Christians believe that among the hints God has given humanity are the Law; the prophets; God's history of dealing with Israel; the Bible in its entirety; and, most fully, God's Word made flesh: Jesus Christ.

As I mentioned above, one of those "hints"— those special revelations—came to Abraham, who lived in the Mesopotamian city of Ur about 1,800 years before Jesus Christ. God said (more or less), "Listen, Abraham, I know your forebears thought that there were a multitude of gods; but all those gods are really just attributes of who I am. So I want you to know there really is only one God. If you believe what I am telling you, I will make a great nation of you and your descendants; and they will be a light to other nations."

In this way, through Abraham, God set the human race on a different trajectory. Even so, the vast majority of the world had not yet heard or understood that there was just one God. What did God think about those people? I believe that God looked at them, recognized that they had not had a chance to hear, and accepted their yearnings on a different sort of level— on the level that a parent accepts the limited understanding of a small child—with patience and a knowledge that one day they would grow up and understand.

About six hundred years after Abraham, God gave another hint. God called Moses up to a mountain and said, "Let me tell you a little bit about what I have in mind for humankind." God gave Moses the Ten Commandments and hundreds of other laws, saying, "Go back and teach my people this, so they know what I have in mind and what is right and what is wrong." Remember, Abraham did not know all those commandments; yet God looked favorably on him. Now, however, the human race had progressed to a point where God felt it was ready for a little more information and was capable of adhering to a higher standard.

Then the prophets came along; and through them God provided more hints, clarifying God's expectations and describing God's heart and character. Christians believe that around two

19

thousand years ago God gave us the clearest hint of all, when God's Word became a human being and lived among us. We believe that, in Jesus, God came to us in human flesh so that we might see and understand God's heart, God's character, and God's will for our lives.

Christians believe that in Jesus Christ we have the definitive revelation of God. We judge all other revelations—from any other faith, place, book, or prophet—in light of the moment when God became one of us. In Jesus' words, "I am the way, and the truth, and the life" (John 14:6) and "The Father and I are one" (John 10:30), we hear the truth that, at a particular time in history, God sought to speak in a way we could understand more fully. God spoke the language of humanity in order to be known. Christians have spent the last two thousand years trying to understand the full significance of Jesus Christ for our lives and for the entire world.

We will explore the Christian religious claims in more detail in the final chapter of this book. For now, let us recognize that this belief in the ultimate nature of what God was doing in Jesus Christ leaves us with a challenge in trying to relate to other faiths. How should we view persons who do not accept that Jesus is the Christ? Let's turn now to this question, examining three very different ways in which Christians have answered it.

How Should Christians View Other Religions?

In this book we will focus on five major religions: Hinduism, Buddhism, Islam, Judaism, and Christianity. Let's begin with the numbers. According to the most recent data, there are approximately six billion people in the world. Of these, two billion—or about one-third—are Christians.

Muslims account for 1.3 billion, or about one-fifth of the world's population. Hindus make up one-seventh, with 900 million followers. There are about 360 million Buddhists, who account for approximately five percent of the total. Judaism has approximately 14 million adherents. That is a very small part of the world's population; yet Judaism is central to a study of religions because the two largest faith traditions, Christianity and Islam, are both linked to Judaism. All tolled, these five religions represent about 4.5 billion people—more than two-thirds of the world's population.

In the United States, 77% of the population claim to be Christian, 15% claim no religious affiliation, 1.3% are Jewish, and one-half of one percent are Muslim, with approximately the same number of Buddhists and Hindus. Yet while Christianity grew at the rate of 5% during the last decade, Islam, Buddhism, and Hinduism grew at the rates of, respectively, 110%, 170%, and 237%.

My point in sharing this information is that it makes clear the challenge of the various religions to our theology and understanding of God. Two-thirds of the world's population are not Christians. Hundreds of millions of people, even billions, are faithful adherents of their religions. They long to know the truth. They seek to serve God as they understand God. Presumably God formed all these people in their mothers' wombs, as Psalm 139 notes. It seems fair to say that God knows each of them by name—knows their stories and has heard every prayer they have prayed, even if their prayers have not been directed to God by name. Believing all this to be true, it seems critically important for us to decide how Christians should view other religions. Indeed, our answers will be a reflection on the character of the God we claim to love and serve: the God revealed in Jesus Christ.

In response to the question, I would like to offer three possible views, among many, that might be helpful for you to consider. Here I will be drawing upon terminology used by Dennis Okholm in *Four Views on Salvation in a Pluralistic World*, among others.

The Pluralist Perspective

The first is the "pluralist" view. According to the pluralist view, all religions are equally valid paths to Ultimate Reality (a term that we might consider synonymous with God). Put another way, pluralists believe that religious people around the world are all really saying much the same thing in different languages, or at the very least they are pointing to the same truth.

Some years ago my grandfather and I were having a conversation about religions. He said, "This is what I believe"; and he put his two index fingers together, making a triangle.

I said, "What do you mean, Grandpa?"

He said, "I think all religions are pointing in the same direction, leading to the same place." This was a pluralist perspective.

Pluralism is probably the predominant view in popular culture today. Most people who hold this view do so with a desire to show respect for all faiths—to be open-minded, fair, and nonjudgmental. Some have said that this is a characteristic of "postmodernity." Persons who hold this view might say, "Your truth is true for you, and my truth is true for me."

I struggle with this view, however, for two reasons. First, I do not think it really honors the various faiths. Most Muslims would not feel that we were honoring them by saying that what they believe is as true as what Hindus believe. They would feel, at best, that we did not understand their faith. If we understood it, they might say, we could not possibly believe that Islam and Hinduism are equally valid paths to Ultimate Reality.

The second reason I struggle with the pluralist perspective as it is popularly conceived is that it fails to differentiate adequately between the logic, validity, and merit of various religious claims. If I understand religion to be the human response to spiritual yearnings, needs, and experiences, then I also must understand that some of these responses are closer to the truth than others. In fact, some truth claims are mutually exclusive. That is, if one faith claims that there are many gods while another holds that there is only one, these two contradictory truth claims will be impossible to reconcile without doing harm to one or the other of the faiths. Some who start religious movements are simply wrong in their ideas. Sometimes these religious leaders are deluded. Sometimes their ideas are unhealthy. Twice within the past thirty years we have seen religious leaders start new faiths, claiming to have spiritual insight from God, and ultimately lead their followers to mass suicide. Just because people claim that God has spoken to them and can convince others to follow, it does not make their words true.

I like the openness, compassion, and sensitivity of those who hold the pluralist perspective. I certainly believe in honoring and respecting religious people of different faiths. But I do not believe the pluralist view makes sense, nor does it truly honor the various truth claims of different religions.

The Exclusivist Perspective

At the other end of the philosophical and theological spectrum is the exclusivist view (sometimes called the particularist view). In its most rigid interpretation, this view holds that all who do not accept Jesus Christ as Savior and Lord will be condemned to hell. To the exclusivist, it does not matter whether persons of other faiths are devout, or whether they are

earnestly seeking God, or whether they have had a real opportunity to receive Christ. They believe that unless people learn
of and accept Jesus, God is bound to exclude them from the
possibility of eternal life.

A more moderate exclusivist interpretation might allow
grace for those who have not yet heard of Jesus. Such exclusivists might express their view something like this: "If people
have had no opportunity to hear the gospel, then God will
judge them according to what they could know. But if they had
an opportunity to hear the gospel and failed to respond, then
they will be judged accordingly."

The exclusivist view has been held by a majority of
Christians through the last two millennia. Today it is the position held by a large number of evangelical and conservative
Christians. According to this view, two-thirds of the world's
population will not experience salvation; rather, they will perish because they have not received Jesus Christ as Lord.

Jesus certainly said that "many are called, but few are
chosen" (Matthew 22:14). To me, however, the exclusivist
view seems inconsistent with the way God interacts with people in the Bible. It does not mesh with the very spirit of the
gospel, which tells of God's love for a broken world.
And it paints a picture of God that even a lost soul finds difficult to fathom—a God who punishes two-thirds of the world's
population because they were not born in a predominantly
Christian culture.

Furthermore, it seems to me that this issue relates not only
to the nature of God but also to the character of Christ. Jesus'
overwhelming passion when he walked this earth was for lost
people. He stated clearly that he "came to seek out and to save
the lost" (Luke 19:10). Given what we know of Jesus through
the Gospels, I imagine asking him this question: "What would

you say at the Judgment Day, Jesus, to a person who loved God, who sought to serve God, but never had an authentic opportunity to accept you?"

When I ask this question, I cannot imagine Jesus responding to such a person by saying, "Away from me! For though you fed the hungry, clothed the naked, worshiped my Father, bowed in prayer daily, and sought to submit your life to God, you never personally invited me to be your Savior." This seems utterly inconsistent with the actions of Jesus in the Gospels.

Many exclusivists would point to John 14:6 ("I am the way, and the truth, and the life. No one comes to the Father except through me.") in support of their position. I will consider this verse of Scripture at the end of this chapter.

3. The Inclusivist Perspective

A third answer to the question of the world's religions is found in what is called the "inclusivist" view. This position maintains that God is at work among all people everywhere, even where there is no Christian witness. The inclusivist Christian believes that Jesus Christ is the definitive revelation of God: God's Word made flesh. Therefore, all other religious truth claims must be measured in the light of Jesus. Jesus is the most complete picture of God. His life, death, and resurrection are the good news for all people.

Having said that, however, the inclusivist also believes that God may be actively involved in the lives of non-Christians, too. God has not "written off" these people who do not yet understand the fullness of the gospel. Instead, with divine mercy, wisdom, and grace, God may actually work through their religious practices to seek to draw them near. God sees their acts of righteousness and of worship and their efforts to know, follow, and yield themselves and views these as directed at him. Even if

25

those of other faiths have yet to understand or accept God's definitive Word to them, God accepts the intent of their hearts—that they are reaching and yearning—and God credits this to them as faith. Inclusivists would note that it is Jesus Christ who saves us and that faith is our only prerequisite to salvation according to the Christian gospel. *People of other religions may not understand or have knowledge of the gospel, but their service to God is a demonstration of the fact that they do have faith.*

Inclusivists are not saying that all religions are equally valid paths or that their teachings are all true. In addition, inclusivists do not necessarily believe that all people will be saved; they are not universalists. Rather, they believe that God examines the hearts of people of other faiths; that God sees their true faith in him; and, as was the case with Abraham, that God credits this faith to them as righteousness.

This view is held by a large segment of the clergy in mainline churches. The Roman Catholic Church in Vatican II espoused a version of it. It also has strong support among some evangelicals. C. S. Lewis, among the most respected evangelical laypersons of the last century, held an inclusivist view. This view has been held by some in the Christian church going all the way back to the early church fathers. (For example, one might read Justin Martyr as cited in Alister E. McGrath's *The Christian Theology Reader*.) John Hick, author of *Philosophy of Religion*, wrote that inclusivism "probably represents the nearest approach to a consensus among Christian thinkers today." Hick overstates this if he means all Christian thinkers, but certainly among mainline Christian thinkers this view is broadly held.

This idea of God's mercy and love for those who are currently outside of the Christian faith—and God's willingness to speak to them in familiar terms and symbols—is what I see at work in the verses of Scripture printed at the beginning of this chapter, the story of the magi. For me, this story provides a good scriptural basis for us to use as we consider our next question.

How Is God at Work in Other Religions?

"Epiphany" means "manifestation." On Epiphany Sunday, Orthodox (Eastern) Christians celebrate the birth of Jesus. But Western churches, on Epiphany, celebrate the remarkable story of the wise men being called by God from the East to pay homage to the baby Jesus. Let's delve into this story in a bit more detail.

We often think of these "wise men" as kings, though in fact they were likely the emissaries of kings. The Greek word is *magoi,* from which our term "magi" comes. While in the time of Jesus the term could apply to a number of different kinds of persons—magic workers or sages, for example—the word was used in the East primarily to refer to Zoroastrian priests of the Persian Empire (modern-day Iran).

Zoroastrianism is a faith that shares with Judaism a belief in one God, a belief in a devil, and a belief in what we would call angels and demons. Zoroastrians believe in many of the same moral teachings that Judaism teaches, although they hold to a number of beliefs that are contrary to Judaism. These magi apparently were astrologers; they looked for signs from God in the heavens.

Imagine for a moment what their procession must have looked like. Can you picture them riding their camels? There were not just three wise men. We think in terms of three because the Bible mentions the three gifts of gold, frankincense, and myrrh. But three priests would not have traveled hundreds of miles across the desert by themselves. There was likely a whole caravan with camels and all kinds of animals, and the priests were dressed in colorful Persian clothes with turbans and robes. And they came to Bethlehem because God spoke to them by means of a star.

This story addresses the very issue with which we are grappling. The magi were astrologers who looked to the stars to foretell the future. Nowhere in Judaism does God call people to follow a star. Yet here we see God giving a sign to these priests of another faith, speaking through their own religious traditions in the way they were accustomed to seeking God. God orchestrated a comet or the alignment of Saturn and Jupiter—something in the skies—just so these Zoroastrian Gentiles would listen. I find this amazing! At Epiphany we remember how God reaches out to all people. Why shouldn't this include people of other faiths who are seeking after God?

What kind of people must these magi have been for God to have singled them out? They must have been people of great character and remarkable faith, righteous people who may have been able to influence their society. And look at their response: Because of this star they had seen in the heavens, they were willing to leave their homes and travel for weeks or months to a strange land, bearing with them expensive gifts. They were the kind of people who, upon seeing Jesus in his mother's arms, immediately knelt before him. And in finding this child they had great joy. In fact, the Scripture says, "When they saw that the star had stopped, they were overwhelmed with joy" (Matthew 2:10). They were not Jews. They did not follow the law of Moses. Nor were they Christians, of course. They were likely Zoroastrian priests whom God invited, while they were practicing their pagan religion, to be among the first to see the Christ Child. Although they did not fully understand, they offered Jesus and his parents gifts as a sign of their worship and joy. Wise people who are seeking after God, regardless of their religious background, will feel joy when they discover truth, when they see God in some new and profound way. This story tells me that God was reaching out to people who were not Jews but who had been seeking God. God honored their faithfulness and knew that they would be the kind of people who would respond to the invitation. God spoke in their own religious language, not in the language of Judaism, inviting them to see the amazing thing God had done in Jesus Christ.

I believe that God is not so small as we often suppose. Yes, I believe that Jesus is the only begotten Son of God. I believe that his life, death, and resurrection are God's direct word to us. I believe that Jesus Christ is the Savior and that one day he will return to judge the living and the dead. I believe that by his death on the cross, he purchased salvation for all people.

Yet God also spoke to Zoroastrian priests and invited them to come and see what God had done in Jesus Christ. This is the same God who sent Jonah to preach repentance to the Ninevites in the capital of the wicked Assyrian Empire. Jonah wanted God to destroy the Ninevites for their wickedness; but God told him, "Should I not be concerned about Nineveh, that great city, in which there are more than a hundred and twenty thousand persons who do not know their right hand from their left?" (Jonah 4:11).

This is the same God who showed compassion upon Hagar and Ishmael and promised to make Ishmael into a great nation—a promise our Arab and Muslim friends believe was fulfilled in them. This is the same God who called Cyrus (the Persian king who lived in the sixth century BC) the Lord's "anointed" (Isaiah 45:1). This is the same God Paul said the Greeks of Athens worshiped at their altar "to an unknown god" (Acts 17:23). About this God, Paul noted, even the Greek poets had discovered certain truths: "In him we live and move and have our being"; and "we too are his offspring" (Acts 17:28).

What Is the Fate of Those Who Earnestly Pursue God Through Other Religions?

The great evangelical thinker C. S. Lewis included a powerful scene in his children's novel *The Last Battle*, the final book in his series called *The Chronicles of Narnia*. The scene represents a kind of final judgment. The character is an individual named "Emeth." Emeth has devoted himself, all of his days, to the worship of a false god whose name was "Tash." In this particular scene he comes face-to-face with Jesus, who is portrayed as the lion, "Aslan." Upon seeing Jesus, Emeth realizes that he has been mistaken all his life and that he has been worshiping the wrong god. He falls on his face, prepared for death. Here is what happens next as Emeth describes his encounter with Jesus:

> [He] touched my forehead ... and said, "Son, thou art welcome." But I said, "Alas, Lord, I am no son of Thine but the servant of [Tash]." He answered, "Child, all the service thou hast done to [Tash] I account as service done to me." Then [I asked ... "Are] Thou and Tash one?" The Lion growled, so that the earth shook ... and said, "It is false. Not because he and I are one but because he and I are opposites, I take to me the services which thou hast done to him.... " [I said,] "I have been seeking Tash all my days."... The Glorious One [said,] "Unless thy desire had been for me thou wouldst not have sought so long and so truly. For all find what they truly seek."[1]

This picture of the grace of God in Jesus Christ strikes me as profoundly biblical. It is what I see when I look at the story of Jonah at Nineveh; and of God hearing Hagar's cries in the wilderness; and of God inviting Zoroastrian priests to be among the first to see the amazing thing God had done in sending Jesus, the lion of the tribe of Judah. And this leads us back to John 14:6, where Jesus says, "I am the way, and the truth, and the life. No one comes to the Father except through me." What does this verse mean? How are we to understand it? Does it not preclude the possibility of anyone entering heaven apart from being a Christian?

When I ponder this verse, there are several things that come to mind. The first is a question: Was Jesus, in this verse, trying to teach us about other world religions and about how God will judge faithful adherents of these other faiths? Reading the context of John 14, this does not seem to be its aim. Jesus is speaking to his disciples, just before his death. He is emphatically affirming that he is the Messiah and that when we have seen Jesus, we have seen God.

Nevertheless, he does clearly say, "No one comes to the Father except through me." Some read this sentence and believe it is saying that unless an individual accepts Jesus Christ as his or her Lord and Savior, he or she will be condemned to hell. But this is not the only possible interpretation. I will offer two other options. First, we might recognize Jesus' statement as a simple matter of fact: No one will come before God and enter God's eternal realm without passing before Jesus, since Jesus and the Father are one (see John 17:21). A second way of understanding the text, and one I find more compelling, is simply to recognize that, while the merits of Jesus Christ's death are essential for all persons to enter heaven, it is up to God to apply those merits as God chooses. So if anyone—for instance, a faithful Hindu who has never had the opportunity to know Christ—were admitted to heaven, this gift of salvation would have been possible because of Christ's work on the cross. God could choose to give this gift of salvation to someone, based upon his or her faith, even though the individual did not know to call upon the name of Jesus.

Those who hold to this view would note that we all will, one day, stand before the Lord; and

> every knee should bend...
> and every tongue should confess
> that Jesus Christ is Lord.
>   (Philippians 2:10)

Those who were not Christians, but to whom God has shown mercy, will on that day fall before the Lord, as Emeth did in Lewis' classic tale; and the Lord will raise them up and extend to them his mercy.

For those who bristle under this idea, I might offer a simple analogy. I know a young man in my church who is severely mentally retarded. He has been baptized, but he will never fully understand the gospel. He will not, in the words of Romans 10:9-10, "confess with [his] lips that Jesus is Lord"; nor do I think it likely that he fully understands that "God raised [Jesus] from the dead." Yet I believe this child belongs to God and one day will see and understand clearly in the kingdom of heaven. How is this possible if he has not personally accepted Jesus Christ as his Lord and Savior? This is possible because I believe God, in his mercy, will apply to this young man's credit the work of Jesus on the cross, doing for this young man what he could not do for himself.

We believe the same is true of children who die before they

reach the "age of accountability." They are still marked by sin and are in need of salvation, but how can small children be granted salvation when they have yet to personally accept Christ? They can be granted salvation because God, in his mercy, applies the work of Christ to their lives. Is it not possible that God would do the same for those who earnestly sought him but did not know or understand that Jesus was the Christ?

Some will ask, "If this is the case, why should we do evangelism? Why preach the gospel to those who are faithful adherents of other religions if God may choose to show mercy to them anyway?" The answer to this question is simple. We offer them Christ because we believe God came to all humanity in Jesus. We tell them about Christ because he is "the way, and the truth, and the life." We share Christ with them because he offers the most complete picture of God and in following him we know all the joy of salvation. We offer them Christ because Jesus commanded us to do so.

When we have such a perspective on God and on others, we share Christ in a different way than do those who hold an exclusivist view of salvation. They may share Christ from a perspective that says, "If you do not believe what I am telling you, God will send you to hell." That approach may work for some, but for many people today this picture of God will repel them rather than draw them to God. Instead we can look at the person and say, "I believe God loves you and is honored by your desire to serve him. I would like to tell you what the Christian faith believes about the God that you know and love." Then we can share with the person our understanding of the gospel. Such an approach seems consistent with both John 14:6 and the rest of the Bible; and it paints a picture of a God who is, by his very nature, love.

* * *

I encourage you to wrestle with the questions of this chapter on your own and come to your own conclusions. The point of the rest of the book is to help you learn about four of the other world religions, to understand where their truth claims parallel Christianity and where they contradict it. I hope you will gain a greater understanding of your own faith. I also hope you will gain a sensitivity that will allow you better to bear witness to your faith, so that you can effectively invite others to come and see what God has done in Jesus Christ. With this in mind, let's begin our study of Hinduism, Buddhism, Islam, Judaism, and Christianity.

[1] From *The Last Battle,* by C.S. Lewis (Collier Books, 1970).

CHAPTER 2

Hinduism

You were dead through the trespasses and sins in which you once lived...and we were by nature children of wrath, like everyone else. But God, who is rich in mercy, out of the great love with which he loved us even when we were dead through our trespasses, made us alive together with Christ...so that in the ages to come he might show the immeasurable riches of his grace in kindness toward us in Christ Jesus. For by grace you have been saved through faith, and this is not your own doing; it is the gift of God—not the result of works, so that no one may boast. For we are what he has made us, created in Christ Jesus for good works.

(Ephesians 2:1-10)

Hinduism developed in India. Its name actually derives from the Persian name for India. Hinduism as we know it today was largely shaped by the people we know as the Aryans.

The word *Aryan* means "noble person." For many years, scholars thought that the Aryan people originated in Eurasia, northeastern Europe, or northwestern Asia. Today, more and more scholars are coming to believe that the Aryans originated in India. Wherever they came from, it is clear that these people were warriors; that they were a noble people; and that they were highly educated, with a well-developed theology and culture. They carried that culture and theology with them across Europe and Asia. The Aryans spread to Iran (the name "Iran" derives from "Aryan") and all the way to Ireland (which also takes its name from these migrating people). Of course, as the Aryans traveled, they took their religion with them.

As the religion continued to develop in Europe, the Aryan pantheon of gods, myths, and stories became what we recognize as the Greco-Roman gods (Zeus, Apollo, Aphrodite, and the rest) and provided the basis for the mythological stories we learned in school. The Aryans' language developed into Latin.

In the East, especially in India, that same pantheon evolved into what we know as the Hindu gods. As you compare the Greco-Roman and Hindu stories, you will notice that some of the gods have very similar names, attributes, and stories. In addition, the language that developed in the East was Sanskrit, which is closely related to Latin in the West.

Historical Context

3800–2200 BC	Aryan influence in India
2000 BC	Abraham
1600 BC	Israelites become slaves in Egypt
1200 BC	The Exodus
1000 BC	David writes his psalms; earliest Hindu scriptures are written
500s BC	Jews are in Babylonian exile Bhagavad-Gita is written

---

Of course, the people of India had their own, much earlier tribal faiths; but it was the Aryans who provided the historical origins of Hinduism.

Hindu Scriptures

Hindus regard a number of books from a wide variety of time periods as sacred texts, much as we do with our Bible. However, there are many more sacred texts in Hinduism than in Christianity.

The Rig-Veda, for example, encompasses 1,028 chapters. These epic poems, which are generally about the length of our psalms, include some stories that are clearly mythological and others that are intended to be taken as descriptions of historical fact. Some of the stories focus on describing the gods and their relationship to nature and to humankind. Some describe our human condition and explain the kinds of things for which we should strive. Many of the poems are quite beautiful.

The Rig-Veda is one of four Vedic books. Hindus believe that the gods gave all four directly to Vedic sages. The Vedas were passed down by oral tradition until around 1000 BC, when they began to take written form.

Next came the Upanishads, which are commentaries on the Vedas. Unlike the texts believed to have been given directly by the gods, the Upanishads are held to be inspired by the gods. They are the reflections of the sages on the Vedic text. The first of the Upanishads were written about 800 BC and continued into the period after the time of Jesus Christ.

Finally, Hindus revere a book of poetry called the Mahabharata, which describes epic battles; with more than 100,000 couplets, it is actually the longest poetic work in human history. Within this larger work there is a small story called the Bhagavad-Gita, which is the most prominent of all the Hindu texts. No Hindu home, it is said, is complete without a copy of this text.

The Bhagivad-Gita tells a beautiful story. Lord Krishna, a human incarnation of one of the gods, is on a battlefield with Arjuna, a human being representing all of humanity. Amid the preparations for battle, Arjuna struggles and asks deep questions of Lord Krishna: What is the meaning of life? How should we live our lives? Krishna responds, offering answers that call Arjuna and all humanity to self-sacrifice and the pursuit of wisdom, which promise joy and life. Some of the writings in the Bhagivad-Gita sound very much like things that Jesus said. Some sound like things we read in our Old Testament. There also are some things with which Christians clearly would disagree.

Beliefs of Hinduism

It is impossible to convey the breadth of Hindu beliefs in the space we have here. As an introduction, I will just mention a few Hindu beliefs. You may want to explore others on your own.

One True God

Before I began my research for this book, I had always considered Hinduism a polytheistic religion. By some accounts, there are as many as 330 million gods and goddesses. But Hindus speak of God in the singular, and their sacred scriptures say that there is only one true God.

The Hindu word for God, at least *a* word for God, is *Brahman*. By this Hindus mean that God is above all and yet in all. God is unknowable, beyond personality, holding all wisdom. To be caught up in God is to experience complete bliss. All of life emanates from God, and our soul is actually part of

God. This picture is of an impersonal God. God is a life force but not a personal being.

Yet there is a second, very different conception of God in Hinduism—of God as personal. As Hindus have explained it to me, the multitude of Hindu gods and goddesses in reality are but manifestations of the one God. They represent different ways of knowing the attributes and character of God. Human beings long to know God in a personal way; so Hindus believe that God is manifested to humankind in a variety of forms, such as the gods Vishnu and Shiva.

It is true that Hindus will worship before statues of gods. Worshipers offer sacrifices to each god. But the informed Hindu believes that all these are really just different manifestations of the one God. Thus it is in the stories of the various gods that Hindus begin to see God in more personal terms. The stories of how these gods interact with one another and with human beings are all meant to help people understand and connect with God. For spiritually mature Hindus, these manmade representations are meant to function much as icons do in the Orthodox churches. In these Christian traditions, icons are portals to God, windows through which believers can see spiritual truth, not objects of worship themselves.

The Human Condition

Hinduism holds that the human soul—which actually is God within us—longs to be reunited with God. This God within is known as Atman. Because God is part of us and God is perfect, we cannot be marred by sin. We simply are ignorant. We do not fully understand reality or what it really means to be human.

Anand Bhattacharyya, a leader of the Hindu temple in my community, explained it to me this way: "We are not born sinners, because we have divinity in ourselves. We have the divine spirit in us, through which we can do great things. But we are ignorant of that. That's why we do all kinds of bad things."

So our struggle is not with sin but with ignorance. If we do bad things, even though we have God within us, it is because we do not understand. We do not recognize spiritual truth, and we do not recognize our destiny. We need to gain knowledge.

Dharma

We can find salvation, Hindus believe, in spiritual knowledge that sets us free. That knowledge leads us to good works, or dharma. The word *dharma* means "duty." Hindus are called upon to do their duty in a variety of ways. By doing their duty and pursuing spiritual knowledge, which go hand in hand, they believe they can be released from this life and ultimately achieve nirvana [See below.].

Hindus have access to four paths by which to gain the knowledge that sets us free from doing wrong. The paths are called yogas. A "yoga" in Hinduism represents the effort that one puts forth to attain knowledge and union with God. One path focuses on the study of spiritual principles. Another focuses on doing loving things toward God and offering worship. The third focuses on certain kinds of exercises, both physical and psychospiritual, that can move us from focus on self to focus on God. The fourth path is pursuit of good deeds toward others. When we follow these paths, according to Hinduism, we are reborn with an opportunity to grow again.

Karma

Hindus also believe in the law of karma. Literally, "karma" means "works" or "deeds." Hindus believe that we build up good karma through good thoughts and deeds. We build bad karma through bad thoughts and deeds. If we have more good karma than bad at the ends of our lives, we progress in the next life. Our next life is a direct result of the karma from our previous life. If we do evil, we will bear that burden in the next life. We will learn through suffering until we gain knowledge and choose not to repeat the evil we have done. Throughout this cycle of birth, death, and rebirth, we can learn more spiritually, pursue more of the duty that God has given us, and build up more good karma until, finally, no bad karma remains. At that point, we are set free from this cycle of life and death and rebirth.

Reincarnation

Hindus believe in reincarnation of the soul, the Atman that comes from God. They believe that this essence of God that is placed within us begins its journey as a very simple life form. Then, through a cycle of deaths and reincarnations, we progress up the evolutionary chain until we develop enough good karma to be born as a human being. When we become human, we are born into what traditionally in Hinduism is the lowest caste of society, the outcasts or untouchables. Then, if we fulfill our duty there, and as we gain spiritual knowledge, we can move up the caste ladder until, finally, after many lives, we are set free from the cycle of death and reincarnation. We no longer need the cycle of death and rebirth to be united with God.

As Anand explained, "The ultimate goal of life is to unite your soul with the Eternal Soul. But it's not easy to do that, so you have to go through several cycles of birth and death, and practice yogas [pathways to union with the Eternal Soul which include: knowledge, devotion, action, and contemplation]. Hopefully, with every birth and death we step up the spiritual ladder, and finally we are able to unite our soul after our death with the Eternal Soul, and that's the end of the cycle."

Nirvana

What happens when we finally have attained knowledge and have exorcised all the bad karma from our lives? We receive salvation—moksha—which is a release from suffering and the cycle of death and rebirth. We then are united with God in a state that is called "nirvana." Some Hindus believe this union is complete; in other words, nothing is left of the individual. We become like a drop of water in a vast ocean, our individuality and distinctness forever lost. Others in Hinduism believe there is a sense in which we remain somewhat distinct, perhaps like a fish that dwells in the ocean but is distinct from it.

Differences Between Christianity and Hinduism

With this very basic understanding of Hindu beliefs, let's take a moment to see where the Christian gospel differs from Hinduism.

The Nature of God

In some ways I see close parallels between the God in Hindu literature and the God of the Bible—the God who told Moses, "I AM WHO I AM" (Exodus 3:14). In the beautiful pictures of God in the Hindu scriptures, I recognize pictures of God from the Bible.

At other points, these two Gods seem very different. In Hinduism, God is in everything and everything is part of God. In Christianity and Judaism, God is distinct from the creation. We look upon the creation as God's handiwork, a reflection of the Artist, but not the Artist himself. We are made in God's image, but we are not to be confused with God.

That point is an important difference between Christians and

Hindus when it comes to understanding the soul. Christians invite the Holy Spirit to dwell in our hearts, but we regard our souls as distinct from God. Because of that distinction, we are capable of sin.

In contrast to Hindu beliefs about God, the God of the Bible is never impersonal. Rather, God loves us and longs to be loved by us. In fact, the entirety of the Bible is the story of God's dealings with humankind and God's desire to be in relationship with us. We can know God and have a personal relationship with God that is life transforming. God is the lover, the bridegroom, the heavenly Father.

When I have asked Hindu friends if they feel a closeness to God or any personal connection, the answer I receive is something like this: "I have not gone that far up in the spiritual ladder. Someday I hope to get there."

I find that response interesting. To Christians, a personal, transforming relationship with God is an essential hallmark of our faith. We experience God in different ways; but we believe that, even before we become Christians, we can experience God's presence and have a relationship with God in an intensely personal way. God's Spirit works with us, helping us to achieve spiritual maturity. We do not have to wait until we reach a certain level of maturity to know God. For Hindus, such a relationship is possible only for the giants of the faith, those who are near nirvana.

There is one other difference in our respective conceptions of God. In Hinduism, as we noted earlier, the images and statues are meant to be icons through which one views God. Christians (along with Jews and Muslims) take a very different view. In the Old Testament, as one of the Ten Commandments, we are told not to make idols—images of stone or wood or anything else by which to worship God (Exodus 20:4-6).

Why? I think there are two reasons. First, no image we could make could possibly contain the essence of who God is. Second, I believe God knew that we as human beings tend to forget that images are meant to be icons, and we turn them into idols. We begin to worship the thing instead of the Creator behind it.

The Human Condition and Salvation

When it comes to the human condition and salvation, I see a tremendous difference between Christianity and Hinduism. Christianity teaches that our soul is human, not divine. We were created in the image of God; but our bent, as human beings, is to do the things we know we should not do. We also have a tendency to fail to do the things we should do. We have much good in us, but we also struggle with sin; and we continue to wrestle with it no matter how spiritually mature we are. The answer to our problem is not within us but beyond us. We cannot make ourselves holy and forgive our own sins. We do not need knowledge; we need grace. We need God's forgiveness. We need God's Spirit to help us. We need a Savior.

Likewise, the passage of Scripture cited at the beginning of this chapter, from Ephesians, notes that we are not saved by our works but only by God's grace, as we trust in Christ. In Christianity, our works are in response to God's love and grace and gift of salvation. They are not an attempt to attain our own salvation or to merit the gift of heaven. Christians believe salvation by works is an impossible task.

Though Christian theology differs from Hindu theology in significant ways, as I reflected on Hinduism, I found the concept of karma to be a concept with some parallels in Christianity. In a sense, we hold to something similar. Paul noted it in Galatians 6:7-8: "Do not be deceived; God is not mocked, for you reap whatever you sow. If you sow to your own flesh, you will reap corruption from the flesh; but if you sow to the Spirit, you will reap eternal life from the Spirit."

This points to the very heart of the Christian faith. To put it in Hindu terms, the perfect, holy, and righteous God became flesh, lived among us, and then bore upon the cross all the bad karma of the human race. God paid the price for our bad karma. Then God credited Christ's righteousness—all his good karma—to our account. Our task is to respond, to accept this act on our behalf, and to begin a new life. As a result, we are not reborn again and again until our bad karma is gone. We are not released by our own action. No, our salvation and deliverance come only through God's intervening action in Jesus Christ on our behalf. This is the gospel of Jesus Christ.

What Happens After Death

A final difference between Christianity and Hinduism is that Christians believe human beings die only once; after that, we face God. This means, on the one hand, that we need to get things right in this life. We do not have multiple chances. It also means that, at our death, we hope to see Christ and those we love face-to-face.

Christianity does not teach reincarnation. In recent years, Hollywood has become enamored with reincarnation; but I have been a bit perplexed by its appeal. In fact, I find the idea of reincarnation discomforting. When this life is over, I do not want to come back and do it again, with no recollection of my past life, without those who have been my companions on the way. I do not want to think that I might return, bump into my loved ones, and not even know them. I look forward to exploring the joys of heaven with my wife, though our life together will be somehow different than it is here. I am grateful that, when I bury a child or a parent, I can say to the family that they will see their loved one again one day.

The picture of heaven painted in the Book of Revelation and in the words of Jesus offers us great joy and hope. When we stand before God, we will be asked, "What did you do to deserve my grace?" Here is the answer: "Nothing. I didn't do enough to build up any good karma from you. I am only saved by your mercy and love. So I'm only holding on to your grace, your forgiveness, and your righteousness, and to the work that Jesus did for me."

And God will say, "Welcome, my child. Enter your rest."

Christians believe that when we die, we are not united with the divine Brahman like a drop of water in an ocean. Our soul is distinct from God. So we have a chance to see God face-to-face, to be known and to know those who have gone before us to celebrate in the kingdom of heaven. We will know that place where God shines like the sun and the river of life flows to the center of the kingdom of heaven. That is the hope we have as Christians.

* * * *

At the time I began preparing this chapter, I had an opportunity to visit a family whose twenty-eight-year-old son had recently been killed. As I was driving to their home, I prayed that God would help minister through me and care for this family.

Then I started thinking, *What would I offer them if I were a Hindu priest? What would I tell them would become of their son?*

I could say, "Your son will come back to try to learn his spiritual lessons. If he has more bad karma than good, his next life might be a little harder than this last one. You, his family, will never know him after he is reborn. But you can take comfort in knowing that, one day, after a long series of births and deaths and rebirths, he will be reunited with the divine Brahman."

That is not what I told this family when I came to their home. I said, "Your son belonged to Jesus Christ. He was not perfect. But all of Christ's righteousness [a Hindu would say his "good karma"] was credited to your son. Jesus bore your son's sin on the cross. And there will be a day when you will see your son again, face-to-face. Until that time, your son is seeing the things we only dream about on this side of eternity."

Being able to say that made me very, very glad that I am a Christian.

I can tell you that I have a great appreciation for Hinduism. There are many beautiful aspects to it. There is much spiritual wisdom in the Hindu scriptures, and Hindus have discovered many things that our prophets have discovered. The Hindu people I have met are hospitable, caring, and gentle. Their emphasis on duty and pursuing goodness, their desire to pursue a course of action called non-injury, their love of quiet prayer and meditation—all these things I find to be profound. We share many truths in common.

Yet at the heart of our two faiths are very different pictures of the human endeavor and our ultimate destination.

CHAPTER 3

Buddhism

I consider that the sufferings of this present time are not worth comparing with the glory about to be revealed to us....We know that all things work together for good for those who love God, who are called according to his purpose.

(Romans 8:18, 28)

Do not worry about anything, but in everything by prayer and supplication with thanksgiving let your requests be made known to God. And the peace of God, which surpasses all understanding, will guard your hearts and your minds in Christ Jesus.

(Philippians 4:6-7)

Buddhist beliefs vary quite widely, and Buddhist philosophies are subject to very different interpretations. Were you to ask the same question of members of various Buddhist groups, you would get slightly different answers, just as you might if you posed a theological question to Christians of different denominations. Below is an overview of Buddhism in general that I think you will find useful as we continue to wrestle with some of the questions people ask about Christianity and world religions.

The Story of the Buddha

Buddhism begins with the story of a man named Siddhartha Gautama. He was born in approximately 563 BC in what is modern Nepal. Siddhartha's father was a prince who ruled a small kingdom. Siddhartha's mother died just after his birth. His father was very protective of his son and wanted to make sure that Siddhartha avoided suffering and experienced only the best things that life offered. So Siddhartha lived in the lap of luxury. At the age of sixteen he married, which was not uncommon in that day, and later had a son. By the time he was twenty-nine, Siddhartha was struggling, trying to understand

---

Historical Context

2000 BC	Abraham
1200 BC	Moses
1000 BC	David's rule
900 BC	Wisdom Literature of the Old Testament begins to take shape
586 BC	Jewish people enter into Babylonian exile
563 BC	Siddhartha Gautama is born
530–480 BC	Much of the Old Testament, as we have it today, is written or edited
483 BC	Siddhartha dies
4 BC	Jesus is born
AD 29	Jesus is crucified
4 BC–AD 29	The Pali Canon—collection of Buddha's sayings and stories about him—is written
AD 700	Development of Tibetan Buddhism

---

who he was and seeking to find his place in the world, much as many of us have done.

In understanding Siddhartha, it is important to understand the religious world in which he lived. Hinduism, the dominant faith in India, had been developing for centuries when Siddhartha was born. Characteristic of the Hinduism of his day, ordinary people of India felt they had little direct access to God. God was viewed as beyond all comprehension.

Members of the priestly caste, known as Brahmans, were the mediators with God. Hindus of the other castes, including Siddhartha's family who belonged to the warrior caste, could approach God only through a priest. The priest would enter into an elaborate array of rituals and services to the gods in order to achieve a measure of good karma on behalf of the petitioner. Apart from this type of request, Hindus tried to build up good karma by living a righteous life and doing the right things. It was unlikely that Siddhartha or his family would have had a personal faith or experience of God. Siddhartha's search for answers to his life questions took place against this backdrop.

There is an important story from Siddhartha's life. Some regard it as historical; others view it as apocryphal. Either way, the story is critical for understanding Buddhism. At age twenty-nine, Siddhartha decided to journey away from his father's home to explore the city. He rode off in his chariot, searching for truth.

He first came upon a decrepit old man, bent over from age. Upon seeing this man, Siddhartha was troubled. His father had shielded him from suffering. Siddhartha had never seen anything like this before. He asked his charioteer, "Is this the fate of all people?"

"Yes, Siddhartha," replied the charioteer. "All of us grow old."

This news was troubling to Siddhartha's spirit, and he began to think about it. Several days later, Siddhartha ventured out into the city again. This time he saw a man who appeared very ill, almost at the point of death. Again Siddhartha asked his charioteer, "Is this the fate of all people? Do we all get sick like this?"

The charioteer replied, "Yes, all people suffer illness."

Siddhartha was troubled even more deeply now. He became downcast. He felt anxiety and even despair.

A few days later, Siddhartha's charioteer took him out of his father's palace one more time. This time they saw a funeral procession going by. Siddhartha had never seen a dead body before. The reality of death had never sunk in for him. Again Siddhartha asked, "Is this the fate of all of us?"

The charioteer again replied, "Yes, it is the fate of all people to die."

Siddhartha had faced the realities of aging, illness, and death. In doing so, he experienced what existentialist philosophers call "angst," a dread or anxiety about the apparent pervasiveness of suffering.

Each of us has moments when we come face-to-face with the transience of life, our own mortality, and the mortality of those we love. The experience can be overwhelming.

I vividly remember the first time I experienced this type of angst. I was sixteen years old. I woke up one morning and stood in front of the mirror, and for the first time the thought struck me that someday my body would be buried in the ground. Everything I ever had, all that I ever experienced, would be laid to rest with me. Even though I knew people died, this sudden realization almost took my breath away.

Sometimes we experience this angst as we are growing older. My daughters love to point out that my hair is turning gray and that a little bald spot is forming on the back of my head. Once when they were talking about this, I thought, *My grandkids will never know that my hair used to be auburn. They'll only know me as their bald grandfather!* We may laugh about hair loss, but there are moments as we age when we feel some of the angst that Siddhartha experienced. We feel it when loved ones pass away and we realize that we will never again see them in this life.

How do we live in a world where we have this kind of angst? How do we live with the despair, anxiety, and suffering that are all around us? Everything is transient. Nothing is permanent. Nothing will be with us forever. How do we live burdened with that kind of knowledge? That is what Siddhartha wondered as he searched for truth.

When he returned to his palace, his father saw Siddhartha's anxiety and sought to help him. He suggested throwing a huge party to chase away his son's despair. But nothing helped. Siddhartha already had possessed everything a person could want in the way of material things. In fact, the inability of material pleasure to reduce his angst led to even greater despair. So, one night, as his wife and son were sleeping, Siddhartha gazed upon them one last time and then left the palace—and his life of prosperity—to seek the answers to human suffering.

Christians seek such answers through faith in God, the good news of Christ, and the peace of the Holy Spirit. But Siddhartha had no access to these. God was an impersonal life force, hidden behind hundreds or even thousands of lesser deities, all carefully managed and served by the Brahman priests. Siddhartha could not experience a personal relationship with God. So he found no comfort from religion.

Siddhartha had grown up in the lap of luxury. He knew that the pleasure of material possessions could not take away this kind of suffering. So he tried the opposite approach. He pursued extreme asceticism. He entered the monastic life. Choosing to fast and deny his body, he eventually came to eat only one grain of rice a day. Finally, on the verge of starvation, he realized this self-denial had not eliminated his angst.

Siddhartha then pursued a middle path, an answer somewhere between pleasure and asceticism. Still he found no comfort. Finally, six years after he began his journey, now age thirty-five, Siddhartha Gautama had a profound revelation, an insight that would at last help him let go of his angst. While meditating one day under a tree, he fell into a deep trance, seeing the world in a way he never had seen it before. When he awoke, he came to understand what he believed was the source of suffering and the path to overcoming it. More than this, he let go of all the things that lead to suffering. Siddhartha reached enlightenment. The Pali word for enlightenment is *budh*. Siddhartha had become the Buddha—the Enlightened One.

He would spend the next forty-five years teaching others what he had learned: a philosophical and meditative system that was meant to free human beings from suffering in this life and to deliver them from the prison of endless reincarnations. The Buddha did not claim to be a god; he was merely a man who had insight into the nature of suffering and the remedy for it. At the age of eighty, he died. Many followers carried forward his teachings.

Essential Buddhist Beliefs

What was it that Siddhartha learned during his revelation that alleviated his suffering and the sense of angst? What beliefs do Buddhists hold? We have space to cover only a few of the most important tenets briefly.

Non-Theism

When we consider essential Buddhist beliefs, it is important to note that Buddhism is the only major religion that is officially non-theistic. It is not atheistic; Buddhists do not maintain that there is no God. The Buddha simply said that the question of God's existence is irrelevant for ending human suffering. Based on the Buddha's experiences, his conclusion is understandable. After all, he turned to the religious deities of his day and found no help. Buddhists neither deny nor affirm God's existence. In most forms of the religion, Buddhists do not worship the Buddha; but they do revere him. They look to him as a guide and example. They hope to achieve the kind of enlightenment that he achieved. With this in mind, let's examine what Siddhartha Gautama learned that set him free from his concern about suffering.

The Four Noble Truths

The enlightenment that came to the Buddha involved certain truths, or precepts, that Buddhists call the Four Noble Truths:

1. *Life is characterized by suffering.* We get sick. Our feelings get hurt. We have painful experiences. We are aware of our own aging and impending death. Life is filled with anxiety and stress. This is not intended to be a dark, depressing point of view, as some misunderstand Buddhism to be. But it is a recognition that life is characterized by suffering.
2. *Suffering is caused by attachments.* Suffering, Buddhists believe, is not caused by external sources but by our selves: our clinging, our attachments. We crave life, so we suffer when we face death. We crave to be loved, so we suffer when love is withdrawn. We crave food, so we suffer when we go hungry.

3. *We can overcome our attachments.* This can be done through renunciation or dispassion or detachment. When we are no longer attached to people or things, suffering ceases; and we no longer need to be reborn and enter another life of suffering.
4. *The Holy Eightfold Path is the way to overcome suffering.* Craving, ignorance, delusions, and their effects will disappear gradually, as progress is made on this path.

The Buddha taught that the source of our suffering in this life is that we have cravings, desires, and a tendency to cling— to attach to others, to possessions, to life itself. I feel angst when I contemplate illness, old age, and death. The Buddha would say that I fear growing old because I long to hold on to youth. By having an attachment to remaining young, clinging to something that is transitory, I will experience suffering as I grow old. If only I could let go of these cravings and rightly train my mind to see all things as impermanent, I might no longer feel pain. I might find peace and joy.

How does one go about becoming unattached to people, places, things, hopes, and desires? According to the Buddha, it happens through meditation and the Holy Eightfold Path.

The Holy Eightfold Path
What is the Holy Eightfold Path to salvation?

Right views
Right intention
Right speech
Right action
Right livelihood
Right effort

56

Right mindfulness
Right concentration

Through the first six of these, as in Hinduism, we build up good karma and avoid bad karma. In general, we as Christians would affirm these first six pathways as well. In the last two, we find relief from anxiety and fear by controlling our desires and thoughts—in other words, through meditation.

A Buddhist lama would tell you that these eight qualities should be viewed more as ideals than as absolutes. You strive for them and seek to achieve them through meditation. You do not actualize them until you attain enlightenment.

Karma, Samsara, and Nirvana

While the Buddha did not embrace the theology of Hinduism because he experienced no blessings from it, he did accept some Hindu ideas. He embraced the Hindu view that our good and bad deeds generate karma, a force or energy that is passed on and determines the state we will occupy in the life to come. If we generate bad karma, we may return to the animal realm, or hell or other realms. If we do good, we will be reincarnated in a more positive state, at a higher level. That is one reason why the Eightfold Path is so important to Buddhism: By doing the right thing, you can attain a higher place in the next life.

In addition, the Buddha accepted the Hindu concept of samsara: the idea that, after your death, your karmic force is immediately transferred to a child being conceived in the womb, so you are born again and again and again in an endless cycle. I have found that many Christians find the idea of reincarnation appealing. That raises an important point to remember about Eastern religions: To Buddhists, reincarnation is always seen as something to escape. The goal is not to be reincarnated but to be released from this cycle of death and rebirth and the suffering that it brings.

Lama Chuck Stanford, a Buddhist leader in Kansas City, explained it to me this way:

> We believe samsara is the cycle of rebirth—that we live not just once or twice but countless lifetimes. It's that cycle of rebirth that keeps us stuck in suffering. That's why enlightenment is defined as ending the cycle of rebirth. Translated, the term *nirvana* means "extinction," as in putting out a flame. It refers to the end of the cycle of rebirth. We believe once you attain enlightenment you stop generating karma, and that it's really just waking up to the present moment, seeing the nature of reality as it really is.

Hinduism teaches that nirvana is the union of one's soul with God. Hindus believe that when we achieve enlightenment, after numerous cycles of life, the small drop of God within us is reunited with the ocean that is God and we are absorbed into God. Buddhism, by contrast, says that we have no soul. There is no "you." We have only karmic energy that is transferred to us from our past life and is no longer generated when we are enlightened. Thus, the journey ends with the extinction of any sense of our personal identity. Our energy is united with, or dissipated into, all other energy. We no longer exist. For the Buddhist, this is nirvana.

Differences Between Christianity and Buddhism

I have a great respect for the Buddha. He was a brilliant man and an extraordinary teacher of morality and meditation. Much of what is recorded of his profound words would easily fit as a part of the Wisdom Literature of the Bible. For example, according to Dhammapada, verse 100, Buddha said, "Better than a thousand useless words is one single word that gives peace."

Some of his sayings sound like the New Testament. When I read Dhammapada, verse 5, I hear the echo of Jesus: "Hate is not conquered by hate. Hate is conquered by love. This law is eternal."

A passage from Dhammapada 133—"Never speak harsh words, for they may come back to you"—is very much like one we find in the Book of James in our New Testament.

Christians and Buddhists can certainly find many things on which we would agree, and those things are well worth affirming. In a time when so many of us are living our lives at a frenetic pace, Christians can admire the Buddha's emphasis on meditative practices. We can agree with—and learn from—his teachings about not being attached to things that are not of lasting importance.

There are many points at which the Buddhist and Christian faiths connect. I wish we had time to explore all of them. However, there also are points of significant departure between our faiths. Let's focus on differences in three areas: God, human suffering, and life after death.

God

Where I believe we find the greatest differences between Buddhism and Christianity is at the starting points and presuppositions of these two faiths. Buddha started with a picture of God, drawn from the Hinduism of his day, in which he found God to be inaccessible and impossible to know personally. So he looked for the answer to human suffering outside of God, through the control of human desire and the mind. He did not deny that there may be a God, but in Hinduism he could not experience God or know God to be of any real help in the plight of humans. God's existence was irrelevant to the Buddha.

God is at the very center of Christianity. The first words of our Bible are, "In the beginning...God created...." This is a central assertion of our faith. God created the universe. Everything in it is an expression of God's glory. As a crowning act, God created human beings in the divine image—beings with a soul. Our soul is not God; it is created by God. We are known and shaped by God. We are God's children.

Our faith begins with the affirmation that God exists and can be known—not simply by a priestly caste of people, but by all people. Not only can God be known, God longs to be known by us. God loves us and wants us to reciprocate his love.

Christianity begins with a picture of God painted by the person of Jesus Christ—a God who has compassion for lost people. This is a God who is with us and helps us fear no evil, even when we walk through the valley of the shadow of death. This is a God who came among us to say, "This is what I am like, and this is my desire for you." This is a God who offers us peace in the midst of the storms of life.

God articulated a path for us—not an eightfold path, but a twofold path. Jesus said that the path of life could be summarized in just two commandments: Love God with all your heart, mind, soul, and strength; and love your neighbor as you love yourself (Matthew 22:34-40).

In Christianity, God does not turn away from suffering; rather, he experiences suffering on our behalf, along with the full range of human experiences from birth to death. God chooses, in Jesus Christ, to experience aging, sickness, and death and the angst that comes from them in order to save humankind.

As noted in our last chapter, Christians believe, using the terms of Hinduism and Buddhism, that God bore the weight of our bad karma on the cross and credited to us Jesus' righteousness or good karma. Christianity begins with God becoming flesh to offer us a simple path of salvation that even a child can understand and follow. God sends the Holy Spirit to comfort, guide, and direct our paths. As we yield our lives to God, God works in us to transform and perfect us.

Human Suffering

A second point of departure between Buddhism and Christianity has to do with human suffering. Buddhists focus on suffering as the primary human condition, whereas Christians see it as one of several conditions we experience. Buddhists and Christians also differ in their responses to suffering.

Christians do not deny the reality of suffering. In fact, most of us have experienced the kind of angst that led Siddhartha Gautama on his search for peace. We would agree with the Buddha that suffering is a very real part of life. We all will grow old. Our bodies will die. Likewise, Christians do not doubt that controlling the mind can help calm the anxious heart. We certainly affirm the value of meditative practices. I would even agree with the Buddha that sometimes our disappointment and suffering are caused by clinging and desire.

I remember speaking with a woman who desperately wanted a job that would have represented a big promotion. Her entire concept of self-worth was attached to getting that job. She was certain that she would be chosen. When it did not happen, she was devastated. At this point we might learn from the Buddha, who taught that promotions and jobs are neither permanent nor of ultimate importance and that the way to overcome angst is to overcome our desires. In this sense, nonattachment might be very helpful. If we are not attached to things, then there is no sense of despair when we no longer have them. I can even embrace the Buddha's eightfold path toward extinguishing those desires with right thinking and right motives and right deeds.

In fact, Jesus taught something that sounds very similar: Why do you worry so much about what you will eat or what you will drink or wear? Don't you know your heavenly Father knows you need those things? But seek first the kingdom of God and his righteousness and all those other things will be taken care of (see Matthew 6:25-34).

Note the distinction, however. Jesus did not tell us to be detached. He told us to be attached first to God. Then the other attachments in our life will fall into place. No, we should not be attached to wealth and power and prestige and what people think of us. We should let go of those attachments. But Christians do not see detachment as the final answer to the question of human suffering. Christians recognize that some attachments are from God. We are meant to be attached to friends and family, to spouses and children, even to life itself. In Genesis, we learn that God created man and woman and that it was a good thing for them to marry and be attached (Genesis 2:18-25). Jesus wept over the death of his friend Lazarus, even though he knew he was about to raise Lazarus to life (John 11:1-44).

With all of these good attachments come suffering. We suffer when family and friends die. Sometimes there will be pain in our lives because we are attached to our children. It hurts to lose a friend, as Jesus affirmed.

The Christian answer to suffering is to remember that our lives belong to Christ and that nothing can separate us from him. The Christian answer is found in the Book of Psalms:

Even though I walk through the darkest valley,
I fear no evil;
for you are with me.

(Psalm 23:4)

Our answer is that "the sufferings of this present time are not worth comparing with the glory about to be revealed in us" (Romans 8:18).

There is a further difference between Christianity and Buddhism. We do not believe that all suffering is caused by our attachments. Sometimes suffering happens because people do bad things. Evil in the world is real. Our answer to unmerited suffering is the one Dr. Martin Luther King, Jr., shared in his eulogy for four little girls who were killed in a church bombing in Birmingham, Alabama, in 1963: God is able to bring good out of evil; God takes unmerited suffering and uses it for redemptive purposes.

We know that some of the most profound experiences in our lives involve suffering, and God uses that suffering to transform us. It was because of this certainty that the apostle Paul could write, "We know that all things work together for good for those who love God, who are called according to his purpose" (Romans 8:28)

We do not flee from suffering. We sometimes embrace suffering and give it up to God to use in our lives. The Gospel of Luke says that Jesus knew he would be crucified; and he set his face resolutely toward Jerusalem, embracing the cross, not running from it, knowing that God would use his death to redeem the world (Luke 9:51). When they were persecuted for their faith, the apostles rejoiced that they were counted worthy to suffer for the name of Christ (Acts 5:40-42).

When it comes to the angst that Siddhartha experienced concerning death and growing old, however, the answer for Christians is not to be found in doing the right thing, or in meditating harder, or even in squelching the desires for life and the love of our families. We find the answer in one simple word: *trust*. Relief from anxiety, in Christianity, comes from trusting in the God who loves us. Do you remember what Jesus said just before he was arrested and crucified? He turned to his disciples and told them, "Do not let your hearts be troubled" (John 14:1a). In other words, Don't feel angst at my death. Don't be afraid. Jesus said, "Believe in God, believe also in me" (John 14:1b).

The Christian path to peace is not found through nonattachment but through trust in God, which is most profoundly experienced through prayer. Recall Paul's words in Philippians 4:6-7: "Do not worry about anything, but in everything by prayer and supplication with thanksgiving let your requests be made known to God. And the peace of God, which surpasses all understanding, will guard your hearts and your minds in Christ Jesus." This is where the Christian finds the answer to suffering.

Life After Death

Finally, Christians and Buddhists have a fundamentally different picture of the ultimate destiny of our life essence. For Buddhists, our being is an energy that is passed from life to life. The moment we die, our karma enters another baby in the womb and is reborn. The ultimate goal of existence is a kind of extinction in which whatever is left of one's energy is snuffed out like a candle, dissipated into the universe. When this happens, there is no more "you."

But the Christian says, "No! God intends more for us than this!" The Christian response to death and our ultimate destiny is found in the resurrection of Jesus Christ. It is found in Jesus' words, "I am the resurrection and the life. Those who believe in me, even though they die, will live" (John 11:25). It is, in the words of Peter, a "living hope" (1 Peter 1:3)—an inheritance kept in heaven for us.

This was in fact part of the point of Christ's coming to earth, that through his death and resurrection we might understand a profound truth about life and death: After this life is over, our candle is not snuffed out; nor are we reborn as another human being or ghost or animal. Rather, we—not simply our karmic energy, but our thoughts, memories, and all that makes us a unique human being—continue to exist, should we accept the gift of salvation offered from the Lord. Upon the death of our physical bodies, we enter that place where time has no meaning, where suffering ceases, and the glory of the Lord is revealed. This offers us not extinction, but the triumph of hope. Ultimately, it is the existence of God and the hope of Easter that characterize the very different paths Christianity and Buddhism take to relieving suffering and to offering peace.

We have much to learn from our Buddhist friends. We need to be still and to live in the moment. We need to be more mindful about prayer and meditation. We need to avoid attaching ourselves to all the wrong things. We need to recognize that the world is transient and not get upset about things that do not matter. We certainly have much to learn about nonviolence and justice and righteousness and love from our Buddhist neighbors. But I think we have a lot to offer them as well: We offer hope and peace through the good news that comes from trusting in God and in the promises of Jesus Christ.

CHAPTER 4

Islam

Sarah saw the son of Hagar the Egyptian, whom she had borne to Abraham, playing with her son Isaac. So she said to Abraham, "Cast out this slave woman with her son; for the son of this slave woman shall not inherit along with my son Isaac." The matter was very distressing to Abraham on account of his son. . . .

The angel of God called to Hagar from heaven, and said to her, "What troubles you, Hagar? Do not be afraid; for God has heard the voice of the boy [Ishmael] where he is. Come, lift up the boy and hold him fast with your hand, for I will make a great nation of him.". . .

God was with the boy, and he grew up; he lived in the wilderness, and became an expert with the bow.

(Genesis 21:9-20)

Of all the religions of the world, Islam may be the most important for Christians to learn about, next to their own faith. Today, our world is experiencing a clash of cultures with the Islamic world in ways, and for reasons, that we simply do not understand. Many Christians have little knowledge of the nuances of Islam and its system of beliefs. If there is to be peace in the world, it is very important that we as Christians come to understand our Muslim cousins.

In this chapter I will describe the story of Mohammed, the founder of Islam. I will review some of the basic beliefs of Islam. I will examine two points of doctrine about which Muslims and Christians disagree. And, finally, I will offer you a challenge and an invitation.

The Story of Mohammed

Islam is the youngest of the world's five major religions. As with Buddhism, Islam began with one man: Mohammed.

Historical Context	
2000 BC	Abraham
1200 BC	Moses
1000 BC	David writes his psalms; Hindu Vedas are written
586 BC	Jewish people go into exile in Babylon; at roughly this time, Buddha enters the scene in India
4 BC	Jesus of Nazareth is born
AD 29	Jesus is crucified
AD 49–100	The New Testament is composed
AD 570–632	The lifetime of Mohammed
AD 610	Islam is born as a religion
AD 622	First Islamic state is born in Medina
AD 635?	Quran is compiled from Mohammed's sayings

Mohammed lived from AD 570 to 632. Born in Mecca in what is now Saudi Arabia, he was the founder of the Islamic faith. Let's begin with his story.

Mohammed's early life was marked by tragedy. His father died just before he was born. His mother died when he was six years old. He went to live with his grandfather, who passed away shortly thereafter. So Mohammed was raised by his uncle. His family was respected and respectable, but they were poor. There was no education for Mohammed, who never learned how to read or write. As he grew up, he learned to work with the traders who came into Mecca, a center of commerce. The great caravans would cross the Arabian Desert and end in Mecca.

People came to Mecca not only because it was a center of commerce but also because it was a center of pagan worship. In the city a shrine called the Ka'bah had existed from time immemorial. When Mohammed was growing up, the Ka'bah was a place of worship for the 360 different deities that the Arabian people worshiped. (Later, Muslims came to believe that Adam first worshiped on that site and that Abraham built the shrine there. The Ka'bah is a cube roughly 40 feet high by 40 feet wide by 30 feet deep. In fact, our word *cube* comes from the Arabic *kabah*.)

Every tribe had its own pantheon of gods, and each tribe would come to Mecca to worship them and offer sacrifices. The worship was not always holy or spiritually pure. Mecca at the time, in fact, was much like Corinth in Paul's day, nearly six hundred years before the time of Mohammed. Corinth had been a bustling commercial center with a famous temple to Aphrodite. As Paul noted in his first letter to the Christians at Corinth, there was a great deal of immorality in that city. So it was in Mecca during Mohammed's time.

While a kind of tribal polytheism was the dominant religion, two groups of people in Mecca did not worship the tribal deities but rather sought to live a life that was holy and set apart from the others. These were the Jews and the Christians. They represented a very small percentage of Mecca's population. Mohammed found himself drawn to these people. He was attracted to their Scriptures and stories and to the kind of faith they confessed. For them, there was no other god, only the one God, who was called in Arabic *Al Illah*—"the God" —which was often condensed to "Allah."

Mohammed became a man of deep spirituality. People trusted him. As he worked in the trades, people came to know that Mohammed was a man of his word. Many held him in high esteem. At the age of twenty-five he married a woman, Khadija, who was fifteen years his elder. She was a widow when they met. Khadija had entrusted her business affairs to Mohammed, and he had done such a fine job of managing her affairs that they ultimately developed a relationship and married. They had six children: two boys and four girls. Once more, tragedy struck Mohammed's home: The boys died in infancy. Their deaths deepened Mohammed's longing for spiritual truth.

Like the Jews and Christians, Mohammed came to believe that there was only one true God. He was deeply troubled by the worship of the many idols in Mecca. He began climbing up to a cave on the mountainside that overlooked the city, spending time in prayer. Around the time he was forty, Mohammed had a profound experience in this cave. In the midst of his prayers he fell asleep and had a dream that would change his life. In this dream he saw a spiritual being he later knew as Gabriel the angel. Gabriel woke him; held out a parchment with writing on it; and said, "Mohammed, Mohammed, read this."

"I can't read it," Mohammed said. "I don't know how to read."

"Mohammed, read this," the angel repeated. Then he pressed the parchment into Mohammed's chest so hard that he thought he would die.

Mohammed woke up and found that the words that had appeared on the parchment were written on his heart. Terrified, he went back down into the city to find his wife. "I've either seen a demon, or I've seen an angel, or I'm losing my mind," he told her. "I don't know which."

During the next twenty-three years he would have visions like this over and over again. He came to believe that Gabriel was communicating God's words to him. Mohammed would emerge from his dreams and speak to the people of Mecca. He told them, "A law says 'There is no other God.' Stop worshiping these pagan idols. Turn to God and repent of your ways or else you'll face the judgment." The people of Mecca did not listen.

At first Mohammed had just a small following, consisting of his wife and a few family members. Eventually, some forty people came to believe. When Mohammed came down from the mountainside, he recited for these believers the things that the angel had told him in his visions; and the believers wrote down the words.

Then tragedy struck Mohammed again: His wife died. To make matters worse, a group of Meccans wanted to kill Mohammed, viewing his preaching on monotheism as a threat to the established worship of idols. About that time, people from a city two hundred miles to the north contacted Mohammed. They had heard about his leadership and offered him the opportunity to come and be one of their rulers. So, in the summer of 622, Mohammed and his small band of followers fled Mecca and moved to Medina. There they set up the first Islamic state. In Medina, Islamic law prevailed, with the worship of Allah alone. Muslims count all time from the "hajjaree," the moment when Mohammed and his followers migrated to Medina and established a Muslim state and hence the rule of Allah; thus the Muslim calendar begins in AD 622. Today Muslims measure time in years AH—After Hajjaree. The book you are reading was published in the year 2005 according to the Gregorian calendar, which is the year 1426 AH in the Islamic world; that is, the 1426th year after the flight to Medina when the first Muslim state was organized. (You may notice that the years do not line up perfectly with the Gregorian calendar. This is because Muslims use the lunar calendar, which has 354 days per year, whereas the Western world uses the solar calendar, which has 365 days per year.)

From the time he established himself in Medina, Mohammed became a political ruler. He was a judge for the city, and he led a small army. He also began to have visions that were very different from those he had experienced on the mountainside above Mecca. Those visions had concerned theological ideas. Now Gabriel told Mohammed how God wanted him to order society, how inheritances should be governed, and what constituted right and wrong in God's sight. Mohammed also received instruction on how to lead an army and wage war—something for which his experience as a tradesperson had not previously prepared him.

As he became a political ruler, Mohammed also became a warrior. He led his band of soldiers on sorties in which they fought against some of the surrounding towns and villages as he and his troops sought to expand their power (and the rule of Allah). At times they warred with the trading caravans from Mecca. They experienced mixed success for several years until a decisive battle took place in which Mohammed defeated the Meccan troops. As a result of this battle, he was able to return to Mecca—now as its ruler. He consolidated power between Mecca and Medina and, ultimately, across the Arabian Peninsula. Upon his return to Mecca, one of Mohammed's first acts was to destroy all the idols at the Ka'bah. Then he consecrated the ancient shrine to the worship of Allah.

Three years later, in 632, he died at the age of sixty-two. Following Mohammed's death, his followers collected all the sayings that had been written down based on the prophet's visions over the previous twenty-three years. They compiled the sayings into the book we know as the Quran. From that time forward, his followers took their faith throughout the world. Within a hundred years of Mohammed's death, Islam had spread like wildfire across North Africa and the entire Middle East and into southern Europe.

Basic Beliefs of Islam

The word *Islam* has as its root the word *slm*. From the three consonants in this word, you may recognize a derivative of the Hebrew *shalom*. Like many Arabic and Hebrew words, *slm* and *shalom* are cousins. "Shalom," of course, means "peace"—the kind of peace that occurs when we live in harmony with God's will and with each other. "Slm" means "peace," too; but it also means "submission" or "surrender." That is what "Islam" means. Islam is the religion of submission or surrender to Allah. A Muslim (Did you recognize the "slm" in "Muslim"?) is "one who is submitted (to Allah)."

Submission to Allah is a profound idea. Obedient Muslims have submitted their entire lives and selves to God. Christians believe in this idea as well—that we should wholly and completely surrender to God. Let's look at some of the other basic beliefs of Islam.

Allah Is God

First, let's address one easy theological issue. Christians and Muslims intend to serve the same God. *Allah* is the word that people use for "God" in Arabic, just as *Dios* is the word for God that people use in Spanish. Clearly, Mohammed was looking at the God of Abraham, the same God Christians and Jews serve. Christians today in predominantly Muslim, Arabic-speaking countries call God "Allah." So do the Jews when speaking Arabic. All three religions intend to worship the same God.

The Quran

Muslims believe that, over the course of twenty-three years, the visions and revelations Mohammed experienced were exactly what he claimed: They were the very words of God spoken to Mohammed by the angel Gabriel. Those collected words became known as the Quran. The word *Quran* means "recitations"; Mohammed, who was unable to read or write, recited the words given to him. Everything that Muslims believe springs from this book.

The Quran is to Islam what Jesus is to Christianity: It is thought to be God's definitive and final revelation. In length, the Quran is about twenty percent shorter than our New Testament; in style and content, it is quite different. Christians believe that human beings who were inspired by God composed our Bible. Our Scriptures are primarily words, stories, poems, and letters about God. Paul, not God, wrote his epistles. Matthew, Mark, Luke, and John—not God—wrote the Gospels. David, not God, wrote many of the psalms. All were inspired by God. But humans did the actual writing.

By contrast, the Quran is all written in the first person—as if God were speaking directly to Mohammed and the human race. The Quran is written in this way: "We say to you, Mohammed, tell the human beings to do this." Or, "We say to you, humanity, do that." Or, "Human beings, don't you understand?" It is a very different kind of text from the Christian Bible.

In addition, for Muslims the Quran is only the Quran if it is in Arabic. They believe that the Arabic words were the actual words that God used. The book is held in the highest esteem. You would never set the Quran on the floor. You would never set it on a coffee table just to gather dust. After all, it contains the actual words of God.

Christians will recognize much in the Quran. There are stories of Adam, Noah, Abraham, Moses, Jonah, Jesus, and John the Baptist. One entire chapter is about Mary the mother of Jesus. But when we read these stories, we find that they sometimes do not match up with the stories we know from our Old and New Testaments. A Muslim would say that where the Quran disagrees with the Christian Bible, the Quran is correct. For them, the Quran is God's definitive word—and the final answer. It corrects the "corruptions" of Judaism and Christianity.

So, what exactly do we learn in the Quran? To understand, we must turn to what are known as the Five Pillars of Islam.

The Five Pillars of Islam
The five pillars are not only teachings but also obligations. In fact, they are the cornerstone of being a Muslim.

Belief. While the Quran is the foundation beneath Islam, the single most important part of being a Muslim is confessing one's faith. In contrast to the creeds that Christians recite, such as the Apostles' Creed, Islam focuses on one simple faith statement: "I bear witness to this truth. There is no God but Allah and Mohammed is his prophet (servant, slave)." That is the statement of faith by which one joins the religion. If you confess this and mean it in your heart, you have become a Muslim.

Prayer. Five times a day, Muslims kneel facing Mecca, bow their heads all the way to touch the ground, prostrating themselves before God. "Our praying is spread throughout the day as a reminder to keep on the path," says my friend Ahmed El-Sherif, one of the Muslim leaders in my community.

Fasting. Once a year, during Ramadan, Muslims fast for an entire month from dawn to dusk. The fast, which is lifted each evening, commemorates the first vision that was given to Mohammed. It also marks the Hijra, the flight from Mecca to Medina. Ramadan occurs in the fall of the year and is based on the lunar calendar; the starting time depends on the appearance of the new moon.

Charity. Muslims must pay their "purity of wealth"—a small percentage of their income that goes to the poor and the needy—once a year. The amount is typically 2.5% of one's earnings.

Pilgrimage. Muslims are to make pilgrimage to Mecca—the *Hajj*—once in a lifetime. If they are physically able and can financially afford it, Muslims are to visit the Ka'bah as a remembrance of Abraham, Ishmael, and Hagar. This journey is a profound experience of unity with other Muslims. "For us," says my friend Ahmed, "the pilgrimage is a remembrance of Ishmael, our father, and our mother, Hagar." Muslims can make the Hajj at any time, but there is one particular month more than others—the month of Hajj—when people make the journey. During this month, people from all over the world travel to Mecca and the Ka'bah.

This is only the briefest synopsis of Islamic beliefs. I wish that space permitted us to delve more deeply into the other beliefs of Muslims. You may want to read more about them on your own. Let's turn our attention now to some of the key differences between the Christian and Islamic faiths.

Differences Between Christianity and Islam

Before describing some differences between our faiths, I must mention that what struck me in my study was the number of ways in which Christians not only agree with their Muslim cousins but also share the same deep convictions. Often, Muslim lives and faith can serve as an inspiration for us. The very name, Islam, means submission (to God)—an ideal that Christians also strive for. Regardless of what they are doing, faithful Muslims stop five times throughout the day and yield their lives to God. They bow all the way to the ground as if to say, "Here I am, Lord." This fivefold time of prayer throughout the day is an inspiration to me and has challenged me to develop a pattern for prayer in my own life. The Muslim way of giving to the poor, setting aside a percentage of one's budget for those in need, is a practice we as Christians would do well to pursue.

Having said that, however, we cannot ignore several fundamental differences between our faiths. I will focus here briefly on these critical distinctions.

Authority of the Quran
As I have noted above, Muslims view the Quran as the actual words of God, the final edition of God's word that corrects

everything that came before it. Christians cannot regard the Quran as a direct word from God. We can read it, admire many of its beautiful passages, and even agree with some of them—just as we might admire parts of any other piece of beautiful literature about God. But we do not believe it is the word of God.

In places, Christians will read the Quran and find that it diverges in major details from our Bible. As described in the Quran, the stories surrounding Jesus' birth, the events that took place in his life, his teachings, and even his death are very different from the accounts we read in the Gospels. The Quran seems to teach that Jesus was never crucified but was taken directly to heaven while another man was crucified in his place. As Christians, we would look at the Quran's version of events and say, "Wait a minute; that's not how the story took place. It's not how the eyewitnesses described it." We remember that Mohammed received his visions hundreds of years after the time of Jesus.

Mohammed claimed that he received direct revelations from God, that God, through the Quran, was correcting the mistaken and corrupted teachings of the Christian church. Mohammed insisted that wherever the Quran and the Christian Gospels disagreed, it was the Gospels that were wrong, not the Quran.

Some television evangelists have attacked Mohammed. They call him a lunatic and slander him in other ways. That is not the way to talk about someone else's prophet. Nor does it help Muslims hear the gospel and our love of Christ. I believe Mohammed was earnestly seeking God and that he was longing to experience God in his life. I have no doubt that he had deep spiritual experiences.

I have come to understand something about how God speaks to us, however. About once a year a church member comes to me and says, "God told me to tell you something." Now, when somebody tells me that, I listen. If God told someone to tell me something, I want to know what it is. At the same time, my "antennae" go up. I think, *How exactly do you know that God told you this and that your own will and ideas are not part of it?* While I do not doubt that God speaks to us and I have often believed God was speaking to me, I also recognize that, as fallible human beings, we sometimes do not hear things exactly as we should.

On numerous occasions over the last two thousand years, individuals have claimed that God gave them new messages that superseded the Bible. They have claimed that God spoke directly to them and appointed them as messengers. In our own country, Joseph Smith made similar claims in founding the Church of Jesus Christ of Latter-Day Saints. Smith maintained that God, through an angel, had given him new scriptures, which became known as the Book of Mormon. Few Muslims would accept that book as authoritative, even though Smith's claims are in some ways similar to those of Mohammed.

I met Christ in a Pentecostal church where it was not uncommon for people to be touched by the Holy Spirit in the midst of their worship. At those times they would stand up and begin speaking a message from God in the first person, as though God were delivering it. This is not unlike what Mohammed claimed to have experienced. But people in the Pentecostal Church believe that sometimes we misunderstand what God is saying. God speaks to us, but we hear God's inspiration and words through the filter of our own ideas. Therefore, we should measure all such messages against what we know of God through Jesus Christ and against the witness of the apostles who knew Jesus firsthand. What does not agree with the New Testament accounts we set aside.

Sometimes even the saintliest people from my little Pentecostal church would get the message slightly wrong.

I remember hearing once of someone who stood up in the middle of a worship service and said, "Thus sayeth the Lord: 'As in the days of *Moses*, when I caused it to flood upon the earth for forty days and forty nights....' " Several young people sitting off to the side whispered, "I wonder if the Lord forgot that *Noah* was in the Flood, not Moses!" Imagine for a moment that every time someone in that Pentecostal church had said, "Thus sayeth the Lord," the words they spoke had been carefully written down. Imagine that all those words over the course of twenty-three years had been compiled into a book and presented as the newest, most definitive testament, superseding the Old and New Testaments. How many Christians would give up their Bibles and replace them with this newest testament? No one would do this; we recognize that our visions and dreams and intuitions of God speaking to us are not on a par with the Old and New Testaments. We recognize that we are fallible and that we might not perfectly understand what God is trying to say to us. Likewise we might wonder how many Muslims would give up their Qurans upon hearing that a contemporary Muslim was claiming to have new words from Gabriel the angel. Not many, I suspect. Yet, from the point of view of Christians, that is just what Muslims are asking us to do when they claim that the Quran is God's final word and that it supersedes the Old and New Testaments.

How Does God Speak to Human Beings?

As I prepare my sermons each week, I pray, "God, open my heart and my mind to hear from you. Please help me to hear your word. Help me to know what you want to speak." But I will not stand in the pulpit and say that "God told me" to tell my congregation this or that. What I can say about my sermons is that I have prayed about each sermon, that I have reflected upon and studied the Scriptures, and that I believe God has led me to share this message with others. At the same time, I must recognize my own fallibility in hearing from God.

So the question for us is, "How does God speak to human beings?" Muslims believe that God spoke a direct, definitive word by means of an angel to Mohammed. Christians, on the other hand, believe that human beings hear God's word through a filter.

We all have filters through which we hear God. For example, after a church service people will sometimes repeat something they heard in my sermon and tell me, "I really loved what you said about...." And I think, *I didn't make that point. I didn't even* want *to make that point. I don't even believe that.*" Yet somehow that is the point they heard. This is part of our human condition. We do not always communicate clearly. We do not always hear things as the speaker intended; we interpret them through our own filters of belief and experience. Until Christ came, God spoke through people, who heard God's word in the light of their own historical and cultural context. But when God wanted to speak a definitive word, it did not come filtered through the mind and heart of a prophet; and it was not offered through the words of an angel. Instead, God became flesh and lived among us.

Because the Word took human form, God could speak to us in our own language. Through Jesus' teachings and life—his love for people, his miraculous healing acts—something about God's nature was revealed to us. When Jesus died on the cross, he taught us about our own sinfulness and the price that God was willing to pay so that we might be reconciled to God. When Jesus rose from the grave, God was teaching us something about death and life, hope and joy. All of this was possible because God became flesh. God did not commit this word to another prophet; God acted directly by living among us. That is what Christians believe. And that is a significant difference between our faith and the faith of Muslims.

A Step Back?

One other word about the Quran. As I read it, the book struck me as a step back from the New Testament, a retreat from the lofty perch of New Testament ethics toward the Old Testament prophets or the judges. It is a step back toward some of the war and violence that we find in the Hebrew Bible but which is spoken against by Jesus' own ethical teachings. Mohammed was a warrior; leading an army was one of the roles he played. So the Quran speaks of not sparing the sword when enemies attack you and killing them all if necessary. Those teachings were a reflection of the violent times in which Mohammed lived.

The teachings of the Quran stand in marked contrast to those of Jesus, who commanded his followers to love their enemies, turn the other cheek, and take up their cross. The teachings contrast sharply with those of the apostle Paul, who advised Christians to bless those who persecute them and to repay evil with good, in order to change the hearts of others and transform enemies into friends. Of course, before Christians become too self-righteous, let's not forget that our own Bible in parts of the Old Testament advocates violence as a response to our enemies and that at times such violence is commanded by God. For example, after their showdown on Mount Carmel, Elijah killed the 450 prophets of Baal. In the Book of Joshua, the Israelites are commanded to slaughter men, women, and children among the unbelievers. In the New Testament we find a very different picture of God. In the Quran I find only the God of the Old Testament.

Islam on Jesus

As we read the Quran, we discover that Mohammed received a very different revelation concerning Jesus than did Jesus' disciples and the apostle Paul. Muslims regard Jesus as a prophet, perhaps the greatest prophet after Mohammed himself. After they say his name, they reflexively add, "Peace be upon him," just as they do when they say Mohammed's name.

Yet, while Muslims believe that Jesus was born of the virgin Mary, was a miracle worker, and was the Jewish Messiah, they do not think that he was in any sense the Son of God. They think he was a prophet. I find this combination of belief and unbelief about Jesus fascinating. Mohammed accepted the idea of the virgin birth but not the reason *for* that birth. In Jesus Christ, humanity and divinity came together; God took on human flesh. That is the whole point of the virgin birth. Why believe in the virgin birth if you do not believe in its message? Likewise, Mohammed rejected the idea that Jesus came to die for the sins of the world. Instead, Mohammed believed that God forgives us when we sin and counts good deeds in our favor; we do not need someone to die for us. But that belief ignores the very meaning of Jesus' name, "God saves (his people from their sins)."

In reading the Quran, some Christian scholars have suggested that Mohammed did not completely understand the claims of the Christian faith. At one point, for example, he seems to have thought that Christians worship three gods: Allah, Mary, and Jesus. At other points he seems to have thought that Christians teach that God had intercourse with Mary and claimed that in this way Jesus was divine. In other places Mohammed, like many, seems to have believed that the Christian doctrine of the Trinity was a form of polytheism (though he himself admitted that there is a Holy Spirit).

In some ways, Mohammed sought to make the gospel easier for non-Christians to believe. In the process, however, he eliminated the central focus of the gospel. To him, Jesus was not God's Word made flesh. Jesus would not have said at the Last Supper, "This is my body, broken for you, and this is my blood, shed for you" because, according to Islam, we do not need a savior; rather, we are saved by the grace of God and by the pursuit of holy deeds. Jesus had no crown of thorns placed upon his brow, nor was he crucified for us. Someone else, Mohammed believed, was executed in Jesus' place. And, of course, if there was no Crucifixion, there was no Resurrection. Even though Jesus' closest companions said they saw him after he had been raised from the dead and were willing to testify to this truth with their very lives, Mohammed rejected this idea.

Christians through the ages have viewed Islam as a distortion of both the Old and the New Testament, a new interpretation of these books that significantly changed and deconstructed their teachings. Christians have not denied that there are excellent teachings in Islam. However, just as Muslims claim that both Jews and Christians corrupted the teachings of Moses and Jesus, Christians believe that the Quran is a corruption of the Old and New Testaments that essentially robs the gospel of its power. According to the teachings of Islam, Jesus was not the Word made flesh. He did not die on the cross for the sins of the world. He was not resurrected to give us hope and life. He was a prophet and a teacher.

On these points, my Muslin cousins and I will always agree to disagree. As a Christian, I look at the Quran and believe that, as is the case with countless other things written by people of faith over the centuries, the Quran got some things right and that some things were shaped by the ideas, cultural context, and theology of Mohammed and the early Muslims. I will honestly listen for what I can learn from their beliefs. But I will always measure those beliefs by the overriding standard that God's definitive Word became flesh in Jesus Christ.

An Invitation...

When we think of Muslims, unfortunately many of us today think of Muslim extremists. But that is not what I think of, because of the time I have spent talking and even attending worship with Muslims and because of the love with which they have greeted me. As I did research for this chapter, visiting their mosques, I was welcomed with open arms. I can only pray that our Christian congregations would welcome Muslims with the same warmth. There is much for us to learn from our Muslim cousins. The extremists represent an extremely small percentage of all Muslims. Yet it must also be acknowledged that the roots of warfare are an historic part of the Muslim tradition and are clearly attested to in the Quran.

I want to conclude by returning to the words of Ahmed El-Sherif. I feel a genuine love for this man; his heart is humble, his spirit gentle, and his devotion to God evident. I asked him to talk about Muslim extremism. He provides an important perspective:

We have our bad apples, and I'm not proud of it. But we don't have a monopoly on extremism; that exists in every group. On the other hand, there are areas in Islam that are sources of friction, and the more dialogue we have and the better we get to know one another, we can reduce this friction.

His opening comment, I thought, was quite important. We Christians know a few bad apples in our own faith. If we examine our own history, we will read about how Christian Crusaders went to the Holy Land and slaughtered those of other faiths. They wrote letters back to their families in Europe, proud that the blood of the Muslims ran as high as the ankles of the horses through the streets of Jerusalem.

... and a Challenge

I want to end with a challenge to you. First, allow me to reiterate that as a Christian I cannot accept the teachings of Islam and the Quran at face value. I have offered a Christian perspective on the nature of the religious experiences Mohammed had and the way I understand the revelations that he believed were from God. Having said that, I see Muslims as our cousins. We worship the same God, though they understand God in ways very different from ours. I believe that Muslims who are deeply devoted to God and have sought to love God and to pursue the highest ideals of the Quran have much to teach us about surrender to God, respect for the Scriptures, and the integration of faith into every part of our lives. In many ways, we could be ashamed of our prayer lives in comparison with theirs. Many Christians fail to give 2.5% of their income to the poor and, as a result, fail to follow Jesus' teaching, "I was hungry and you gave me food" (Matthew 25:35) as fully as our Muslims cousins.

We as Christians also have much to share with Muslims about Jesus Christ and what he can do in our lives. The question is how we will share this. By arguing? By reacting fearfully? By judging them without getting to know them? By avoiding them because they are different?

The only way I believe we can share the gospel with our Muslim neighbors is by reaching out in love toward them.

I think that sentiment was captured well by my friend Ahmed. It also serves as an invitation to you:

> Muslims are probably as frightened as anybody else—if not more frightened. So reaching out to them is very important. If you find some of them unable to reach back, perhaps it is due to their fear and the current political crisis. Muslims are good people. They are trusted. They are hard working. They have families.

I would be proud to call a Muslim a friend or a neighbor. We share much in common with Muslims. Yes, there are critical points where we disagree. But we will never help Muslims understand the significance of Jesus Christ if we cannot first let them see his love through us. In 2 Corinthians 5:20, Paul says, "We are ambassadors for Christ, since God is making his appeal through us." Our calling is to be ambassadors to all people, but especially today to our Muslim cousins.

What kind of ambassador will you be?

CHAPTER 5

Judaism

Now the LORD said to Abram, "Go from your country and your kindred and your father's house to the land that I will show you. I will make of you a great nation, and I will bless you, and make your name great, so that you will be a blessing. I will bless those who bless you, and the one who curses you I will curse; and in you all the families of the earth shall be blessed."...

He brought him outside and said, "Look toward heaven and count the stars, if you are able to count them." Then he said to him, "So shall your descendants be." And he believed the LORD; and the LORD reckoned it to him as righteousness.
(Genesis 12:1-3; 15:5-6)

Unlike each of the other world religions, of which I was a novice student, there is a degree to which I feel I have known Judaism all my life. I suspect many Christians can relate to that feeling. I have read the Hebrew Bible cover to cover so many times. As a divinity student I studied these Scriptures inside and out, taking them apart and putting them back together again. I have walked the streets of the Old City of Jerusalem, stood atop lofty Masada, and sailed across the Sea of Galilee.

Perhaps you have, too. I can recount the history of Israel, at least to the New Testament period, from memory. These stories are our stories.

Yet it is precisely here where my knowledge fails; for from the New Testament period forward, I lose sight of the history of the Jewish people, their customs, and their developing theology. From that point onward, my focus has been on the church to such an extent that I know relatively little about contemporary Judaism. Until preparing to write this book, I had never read the Talmud and had spent only a cursory amount of time studying Jewish history since the second century. I still know too little of Jewish traditions. Worshiping at the synagogue always leaves me a bit disoriented. The order of worship is familiar; but the songs, the traditions, the liturgy, even the language (though I studied Hebrew in college) are new territory for me.

In this chapter we will briefly review the history of the Jewish people, including contemporary Judaism. We will explore some questions Christians often have about Judaism. We will examine the one point on which Jews and Christians fundamentally disagree. And, at the end of the chapter, I want to issue you a challenge.

A Brief History of the Jewish People

Judaism is the story of the One God who created the entire universe. It is also the story of a particular people through whom God chose to work to redeem the human race. Buddhism begins with one person, the Buddha. Islam begins with Mohammad. Judaism begins, "In the beginning," with God. And it begins with a family of people with whom God entered into a special relationship, a covenant relationship, blessing them so that they might become a blessing to others.

This part of the story begins around 2,000 BC, when God chose Abraham and his wife Sarah, who lived in what is now Iraq, as the patriarch and matriarch of this nation-to-be. They were called Hebrew people, from the name of one of their forebears, Ebre. These people were shepherds and Bedouin wanderers; and, because of this, others often looked down on them.

Abraham, 75, and Sarah, 65, were a most unlikely couple for God to choose—at least they seem unlikely to us. As we come to learn throughout the Bible, God often chooses the most unlikely people. Maybe those unlikely choices are to remind us that it is not about us; it is about God. God, not us, does amazing, miraculous things.

So God chose Abraham and Sarah, then waited an additional twenty-five years, when they were 100 and 90, to give them a son, Isaac.

Isaac, in turn, had a son named Jacob. Like many of us, Jacob struggled with his faith. Literally and figuratively, he wrestled with God. So God changed his name to "Israel" (meaning "one who wrestles with God").

Israel had twelve sons and several daughters. His children and their descendants became known as the twelve tribes of Israel.

I wish space permitted me to recount the story of the Jewish people as it is told in the Hebrew Bible, the thirty-nine books we Christians call the Old Testament. It is a fascinating tale. Instead, I will summarize it as the great theologian and scholar Albert Outler once did: The Hebrew Bible is the story of covenant-making and covenant-breaking.

God makes several covenants with Abraham, Moses, the Israelites, and King David. God offers blessings and love in return for obedience, trust, and faithfulness. The people willingly enter into these covenants.

Yet the Scriptures record generation after generation who fall away from God. They engage in covenant-breaking. They begin to embrace other gods. They leave behind the laws that God gave them. Nevertheless, God continues to love this people and seeks to save them.

When the people wander away from God and from the covenant that protects them, the surrounding nations attack. The people cry out to God. God mercifully delivers them, restores the covenant, and they start the process all over again. Eventually, the people forsake the covenant again, call out to God again, and God redeems them once more.

This is the story of the Hebrew Bible—from the worship of the golden calf to the conquest of Canaan, from the story of the judges to the struggle of the kings of Judah and Israel to keep the faith— and it is the reason the prophets arose to preach. Israel's history is marked by struggles to remain faithful, times of oppression, and God's covenants and promises to redeem and care for his people.

All this is not just Israel's story, however. It is our story, too. As human beings, we are "prone to wander, prone to leave the God we love." We make covenants and promises to the Lord when we are in trouble or in need; and then, over time, we tend to wander away. God takes us back every time. All of us are like Israel: We wrestle with God.

Major Writings of Judaism

For most Christians, the writings of Judaism are a study in contrasts. As I have noted above, we know a great deal about some of them. About others, most of us know next to nothing. So let's spend a moment examining how Jews tell their story.

The Tanak

The Tanak is the Hebrew Scriptures. It encompasses:

The *Torah*: The first five books of the Bible. We also call them the books of the Law or the books of Moses.

The *Nevi'im* (or the Prophets): Not just the writings of prophets such as Jeremiah and Isaiah, Joshua, Judges, First and Second Samuel, and First and Second Kings are also considered part of the Prophets in the Hebrew Bible.

Ketuvim (or Writings): Psalms, Proverbs, Job, and others.

The word *Tanak* comes from combining the initial sounds of Torah, Nevi'im, and Ketuvim.

The Talmud

The Talmud is the oral tradition that developed in interpreting the law. First and foremost, it includes commentaries, called the Mishnah. Over the centuries, rabbis wrote the Mishnah to help people interpret the Torah for their lives. The rest of the Talmud is composed of sermons, teachings, and anecdotal stories about how to interpret both the Mishnah and the Torah. Altogether, the Talmud runs to more than three million words. The compilations which make up the Talmud, produced over the course of hundreds of years, are found in two different Talmuds, the Palestinian and the Babylonian.

Contemporary Judaism

Judaism is not a monolithic faith. Just as there are denominations within Christianity, there are branches or divisions within Judaism. In the United States there are three major divisions: Orthodox, Conservative, and Reform.

Let's look briefly at each one in turn. Here is how Rabbi Mark Levin, the leader of a Reform congregation in my community, describes the three branches in a nutshell:

Orthodox

"The Orthodox would say that Judaism is God's religion. That is, God gave it to the Jewish people. Orthodoxy believes that the Torah and the Talmud were both given by God."

Conservative

"Conservative Judaism is also called Positive Historical Judaism. They believe that things change over time. They follow Jewish law or Jewish tradition. Like the Orthodox, they regard the Torah as divinely given—but they don't necessarily share that view when it comes to the Talmud."

Reform

"For Reform Judaism, Torah is divine inspiration, and the Talmud was written by human beings. Reform Judaism does not believe that the Messiah is or will be an actual person. Neither does Reform Judaism believe in the resurrection of the dead. But most people do not realize that Reform Judaism has always believed in an immortal soul in every human being."

In this chapter, we will focus primarily on Orthodox and Reform Judaism. Orthodox Judaism is what most of us think of as Judaism. It represents the attempt literally to fulfill the Jewish law to the greatest degree possible today. We think of men with their curly locks and flowing beards, dressed in black. At the same time, the Judaism with which we likely are most familiar is Reform—which also is perhaps the Judaism we feel the greatest ability to connect with. Reform Judaism's approach to the Law looks a bit more like our own as Christians.

The Essence of Judaism

What does it mean to be a Jew today? In his excellent book *The Five Great Religions,* Edward Rice writes, "To lead a 'Torah-true' life—that is the essence of Judaism." But what does this mean? For the Orthodox it means continuing to live the Torah in every way possible, to focus one's life on living by the precepts of the Law. But for many Jews it simply means trying to be decent human beings and passing on several key traditions.

In this way, Judaism is focused on deeds. Christianity begins with a relationship with God, and that relationship transforms us. Our deeds spring forth from the transformation. In Judaism a relationship with God is laudable and is possible, but the primary goal is obedience to the covenant that God made with Moses and the people. Here is how Rabbi Levin puts it:

> Judaism is morality. It's God's revelation through inspiration of how to spend our lives being God's servants. Our mission is to live the life of God if God could do this on earth. But God can't do it on earth. It's not in the nature of God to be able to do it, so God needs servants. By acting correctly in the world, we sanctify God's name. By doing the right thing, people will see that our actions testify to the presence of God in the world. We would never try to convert other people. It's nowhere in the jargon of Judaism. Rather, we want people to come to the conclusion of God by virtue of our conduct and to do what they consider to be the right thing.

If the essence of Islam is bound up in the saying, "There is no God but Allah, and Muhammad is his prophet," the essence of Judaism is captured in what is called the Shema, a word that means "hear" or "listen." The Shema is a passage of Scripture all Jews are meant to have on their hearts and in their minds. You will find it in Deuteronomy 6:4-5: "Hear, O Israel: The LORD is our God, the LORD alone. You shall love the LORD your God with all your heart, and with all your soul, and with all your strength."

This statement in many ways captures the essential belief and life of Judaism. We as Christians recognize it too, because Jesus said of it, "This is the greatest and first commandment" (Matthew 22:38).

Do Jews Still Hope for the Messiah?

Among the questions Christians often ask regarding Judaism is this one: Do Jews still hope for the coming of the Messiah? The answer: It depends on whom you ask.

The Orthodox still pray daily for the coming of the Messiah. They believe that he will restore Israel's sacrificial system and splendor, while ushering in an age of peace. They believe the Messiah will tear down the Muslim Dome of the Rock on the Temple Mount in Jerusalem and rebuild the Temple. From there the Messiah will reign, and the whole world will recognize the biblical God and the truth of Judaism.

Reform Jews have left behind the idea of a literal Messiah. They believe that the passages in the Old Testament that refer to the Messiah are meant to be spiritualized, or turned into basic principles and ideas. They believe that there will be a messianic age, in which peace, righteousness, and justice prevail. And they believe that all of us are instruments through whom God will bring about that age. If we live as God intended, then God will use us to usher in the perfect, messianic world.

Why Do Most Jews Not Accept Jesus as the Messiah?

Perhaps the question most often asked by Christians regarding the Jews is, "Why don't the Jews believe Jesus was the Messiah?" Part of the answer is that the question is wrong. Some Jews *did* believe that Jesus was the Messiah.

All the first Christians were Jews. Actually, they did not call themselves Christians. They were followers of "the Way." They were not starting a new religion; they were being faithful Jews, following the Messiah who had been promised long ago. All but one of the New Testament authors was a Jew. All the apostles were Jews. The founding members of the church were Jews.

It was said that by AD 50—within twenty years of Jesus' resurrection—one-third of the people of Jerusalem were followers of the Way, including many prominent priests and Pharisees. In fact, it was said that, across the land of Israel at that time, there were more followers of Jesus as the Messiah than there were Pharisees, Sadduccees, and Essenes combined.

Nevertheless, most Jews did not believe. As the Christian churches began to move more and more into the Gentile world, Judaism became more closed to the gospel of Jesus Christ.

How that split happened has to do in part with the apostle Paul and his understanding of the gospel. That understanding made it possible for Gentiles to be followers of Christ, but it also alienated many of the Jews of the time. Paul, of course, was a Pharisee and a rabbi. He had been a persecutor of the followers of the Way until he met Jesus, in a vision, on the road to Damascus.

After he became a Christian, Paul—who knew the Hebrew Scriptures thoroughly—began to understand an important passage from the prophet Jeremiah in a new and different way. Hundreds of years before Jesus was born, Jeremiah wrote:

The days are surely coming, says the LORD, when I will make a new covenant with the house of Israel and the house of Judah. It will not be like the covenant that I made with their ancestors when I took them by the hand to bring them out of the land of Egypt—a covenant that they broke, though I was their husband, says the LORD. But this is the covenant that I will make with the house of Israel after those days, says the LORD: I will put my law within them, and I will write it on their hearts; and I will be their God, and they shall be my people. No longer shall they teach one another, or say to each other, "Know the LORD," for they shall all know me, from the least of them to the greatest, says the LORD; for I will forgive their iniquity, and remember their sin no more. (Jeremiah 31:31-34)

Paul remembered hearing that Jesus had said at the Last Supper, "This cup is the new covenant in my blood. Do this, as often as you drink it, in remembrance of me" (1 Corinthians 11:25). Paul saw the connection: Jesus made possible a new covenant between God and us. Salvation was now possible, not by following the Law, but by trusting in Christ, who made it possible for anyone, from the least to the greatest, Jew or Gentile, to be able to follow the God of Abraham. Followers of Christ need not be circumcised. They need not become Jews. According to the new covenant, they need only trust in Christ and begin to live out their faith, following the guidance of the Holy Spirit.

This understanding created a great division in the early church. You can read about it in the Book of Acts. From that time forward, as the church welcomed more Gentiles, who did not have to become Jews, the Jews became alienated from the gospel. I often have wondered what might have happened had

Paul discerned a way to build a bridge, so that Jews could pursue a very Jewish course of following Jesus while Gentiles pursued a "new covenant" course. I have wondered, had that happened, if today much of the Jewish world would be followers of the Way. But that is not what happened.

Jews, then as now, look at some of the messianic promises in Scripture and believe that Jesus did not fulfill them. The people expected then—as the Orthodox do now—that the Messiah would usher in a golden age for Israel. He would bring peace. The Scriptures promised that, in the messianic age, the lion would lie down with the lamb, people would beat their swords into plowshares, and God's glory would be revealed. Because such a dramatic series of events did not occur with Jesus and because the Romans remained as oppressive rulers, many Jews did not (and do not) believe he could have been the Messiah.

How Do Jews Atone for Their Sins Today?

One other question Christians frequently ask today is, "Since they no longer offer animal sacrifices, how do Jews atone for their sins?"

The answer involves the destruction of the Temple by the Romans. In AD 67, the Jews revolted against Rome. The Romans sent some of their finest legions in response, under the command of one of their greatest generals, Vespasian, who would become the next emperor.

In AD 70, Vespasian's armies crushed the rebellion. One million Jews were slaughtered. As a percentage of the population, more Jews were killed then than in the Holocaust. The Temple was totally destroyed. Just as Jesus had foretold (Matthew 24:1-2), not one stone was left atop another.

The law of Moses had required Jews to offer an animal sacrifice as atonement for their sins; but without the Temple, Jews no longer could do so. Increasingly they turned to the Scriptures, which note that "to obey is better than sacrifice" (1 Samuel 15:22). They began to teach that good deeds could atone for bad deeds and that, by pursuing good works coupled with genuine repentance, one could be forgiven.

Christians and Jews

As we prepare to examine the areas of belief about which Jews and Christians fundamentally disagree, let's note that there is so much more on which we concur:

We agree that the first thirty-nine books of our Bible are sacred texts inspired by God; we share those books in our respective Scriptures.

We agree that God is a shepherd, the King of the universe, the Creator of all things.

We agree that human beings were created in God's image and that we naturally struggle with sin (though Judaism does not use the term "original sin" to describe this state). We agree that the children of Israel are the people chosen by God.

The essential statement of Judaism is at the heart of Christianity as well. That is, we, too, hold fast to the truth that God is one and that we are to love the Lord our God with all our heart, soul, and strength.

On one thing we disagree, however; and that is the identity of Jesus Christ. For our Jewish friends, Jesus is a great teacher. He is a rabbi. He might even be a prophet. But he is not the Son of God. He is not God's Word made flesh. Christians look at Jesus and see the Messiah, the fulfillment of the promises of God, and our Savior and Lord.

Why I Believe Jesus Is the Messiah

We have examined one of the reasons most Jews today do not believe Jesus is the Messiah. I want to state why I cannot fathom that Jesus is *not* the Messiah.

Early Christians saw Jesus everywhere they turned in the Hebrew Bible. They saw a foreshadowing of him when the mysterious King of Righteousness, Melchizedek, came to meet Abraham bearing bread and wine (Genesis 14:17-20). They looked back at God's promise to Abraham, "In you all the families of the earth shall be blessed" (Genesis 12:3) and saw the mission to the Gentiles as the unfolding of God's plan of salvation, through the gospel of Jesus Christ, for all humankind.

They saw in the offering of animals to atone for sins a foretaste of Jesus, the Lamb of God who takes away the sins of the world. They read the passages in Isaiah about the prince who was to be born—the son from David's royal line who would be called "Wonderful Counselor, Mighty God, Everlasting Father, Prince of Peace" (Isaiah 9:6)—and they said, "Who else but Jesus could be called by these names?"

When they looked at the Suffering Servant passages of Isaiah 53—the verses describing one who was "wounded for our transgressions, [and] crushed for our iniquities"—they certainly recognized that Israel many times had played that role. The Jewish people had suffered as God worked through them to bring about the redemption of the world. Yet they could never fully explain these passages of Scripture about the man who paid a price for our sin, who received the punishment that we deserved, whose stripes healed us, until they looked at the passages through the prism of Jesus. Those Jews who became Christians began to understand why Jesus did not seek earthly power, why the Son of God allowed himself to be executed like a criminal. Now they finally grasped it: Jesus was not a Messiah who came as a royal prince but one who came to suffer on behalf of God's people.

These early Christians looked at Shadrach, Meshach, and Abednego standing in the fiery furnace for their faith and remembered that in the fire there was one who had "the appearance of a god" (Daniel 3:19-25) who stood with them. And again they saw Jesus, who suffers with us to deliver us.

They read Ezekiel 34:11-16, where God says:

> For thus says the Lord GOD: I myself will search for my sheep, and will seek them out. As shepherds seek out their flocks when they are among their scattered sheep, so I will seek out my sheep. I will rescue them from all the places to which they have been scattered on a day of clouds and thick darkness. I will bring them out from the peoples and gather them from the countries.... I myself will be the shepherd of my sheep, and I will make them lie down, says the Lord GOD. I will seek the lost, and I will bring back the strayed, and I will bind up the injured, and I will strengthen the weak.

They read that passage and could not help but remember how Jesus looked upon people with compassion, how he said they were like sheep without a shepherd. They remembered how many times he sat at supper with sinners and tax collectors and prostitutes and how he said, "I am the good shepherd. The good shepherd lays down his life for the sheep" (John 10:11).

The early church leaders also remembered what Jesus had said about himself. They recalled how he read the scroll from Isaiah in the synagogue at Nazareth:

> The Spirit of the Lord is upon me,
> because he has anointed me
> to bring good news to the poor.
> He has sent me to proclaim
> release to the captives
> and recovery of sight to the blind,
> to let the oppressed go free.
>
> (Luke 4:18)

and then said, "Today this scripture has been fulfilled in your hearing" (Luke 4:21).

All Judaism holds the hope of eternal life in one form or another. The Orthodox believe in resurrection. Reform Jews believe there is an immortality to the soul. You will not find that belief explicitly stated in the Hebrew Bible; only a couple of passages hint at it. So how else would God speak the final, determinative word to give us hope in the face of death? Jesus said, "I am the resurrection and the life. Those who believe in me, even though they die, will live, and everyone who lives and believes in me will never die" (John 11:25-26). God demonstrated this truth through the resurrection of Christ.

When I read the Hebrew Scriptures, as much as I love them, I find they are incomplete apart from Jesus. Christians believe that, in Jesus, God put on human flesh so that we can have direct access to God—so that, through Jesus, we can see, know, and understand God, realizing that God has done for us what we cannot do for ourselves. That is, God sent his Son to suffer for us, to die for us, and to be raised from the dead for us.

Finally, I cannot help but wonder how the history of Judaism might have been different, at least in the first and second centuries, had the Jews of that day not sought a political messiah who would overthrow the Romans with a sword and return Israel to some golden period. How might history have changed had they understood that God was concerned with the salvation of the world and that this would not be accomplished with the sword but with the gospel that, in AD 312, would lead the Roman emperor Constantine to become a Christian. How would the fate of those Jews have been different had they been looking for this kind of messiah—had they sought to love their enemies rather than overthrow them.

For me as a Christian, Jesus represents the fulfillment of the promise made to Abraham four thousand years ago. It was through this offspring of Abraham that all the nations of the earth would be blessed. It was through this offspring that Abraham's descendants would be as numerous as the stars in the sky. And it was through this descendant of David that a king would rule forever. He was born, as Paul said in Galatians, in "the fullness of time" (Galatians 4:4). At just the right time in human history, God sent forth Jesus, "born under the law, in order to redeem those who were under the law" (Galatians 4:4-5). Just a few decades before the Temple was destroyed and animal sacrifices effectively abolished, Jesus came so that he could be the final, atoning sacrifice. I believe this timing was no coincidence. When I read the Hebrew Bible, even in the light of critical scholarship, I too see Jesus everywhere in this book. I believe he is the fulfillment of God's covenants.

I believe that God chose to become human and live among us to help us recognize that we are covenant-breakers more than we are covenant-makers. God said, "I'll make a new covenant. I'll show you who I am. I'll show you my love. I will set you free."

A Tragic Past and an Invitation

With all this in mind, how can I not wish that my Jewish friends would see in Jesus their Messiah? I wish that they could reclaim the early faith of James and John and Peter and Mary and Martha and teach the rest of us about our Jewish heritage. I am aware that there are synagogues of "Messianic Jews" who believe in Jesus, but most rabbis disparage them and teach that one cannot be a Jew and worship Jesus as the Messiah. Yet the earliest followers of Christ all considered themselves faithful Jews who came to know grace and hope through the Messiah of God.

Many Jews cannot fathom this, just as I cannot fathom their contention that Jesus is not the Messiah. So to them I would say, "If you will not follow Jesus, then be an outstanding follower of Moses. Be a great Jew. Be actively involved in the synagogue. Pursue the kind of passionate relationship with God that the psalmists knew. Study the Scriptures. Be the light!"

I am often asked what I, as a Christian pastor, think about the salvation of Jews. I always point to a passage of Scripture, Romans 11:28-29, in which Paul wrote about the Jews. He said, "As regards election they are beloved, for the sake of their ancestors; for the gifts and the calling of God are irrevocable."

That is a powerful passage of Scripture. Paul says that the Jews will always be God's covenant people through the covenant with Abraham, Isaac, Jacob, Moses, and David. This covenant is *irrevocable*. God does not go back on covenants. In other words, while a new covenant has been offered, so long as some Jews do not understand or believe in it, they are still bound by the old covenant, including God's gracious promises and expectations.

Some Christians might point out that elsewhere in the New Testament the old covenant is called "obsolete," and it is noted that one day it will disappear (Hebrews 8:13). But obsolete is not the same as inoperative. I have an old computer that is slow as molasses, has no hard drive, has no modem, and cannot run current software. It is obsolete, but it still operates.

Another contemporary analogy may be helpful for how I view the two covenants of Christianity and Judaism. Several years ago I purchased my first cell phone. I signed up for what at the time was the best deal available: 200 minutes per month for $39.99. I signed a 2-year contract—a covenant—with the phone company. Over time I just used my phone, not keeping up with all the charges, not really paying close attention to my bills, until one day there was a $150 bill. I realized that I had been using my cell phone about 500 minutes per month, but under my old contract I was required to pay so much a minute for every minute over 200. I discovered that new contract plans were available; now 1000 minutes were available for the same $39.99 per month, but I had to request this new plan. I could choose to stay with my old covenant and keep paying higher premiums; or I could enter into a new agreement, a new covenant, in which I would receive 5 times as many minutes for the same price. If I chose to keep the old covenant, I would still have phone service—It would not be revoked—but I would be paying more than I needed to pay and missing out on the benefits of the new covenant.

As a Christian I see the new covenant made possible by Jesus as offering us grace and mercy, joy and hope, life here and now and life eternal—all by faith in Christ and through his redemptive work. The old covenant requires human beings to strive to fulfill the entirety of the law, to atone for one's sins through sacrifice, and to see obedience and good deeds as the means to salvation rather than our grateful response to the gift of salvation. Yet I believe that in Romans 11, Paul opens the door for us to consider that the first covenant is not negated by the second covenant and that salvation is still possible for

God's people the Jews as they seek to fulfill the terms of the first covenant and call upon the grace of God.

Does this mean that Jesus is not necessary for their salvation? No, it does not. As noted in Chapter 1, I am persuaded that it is only by the work of Christ, as our one, complete, and final sacrifice for the sins of the world, that any are saved. He died for the sins of the world. But acknowledging this, and believing that God's desire is for all to accept him, does not preclude God from crediting his saving work to those of his people, the Jews, who have yet to understand or accept Jesus Christ as their Messiah. God will judge the hearts of his people. God knows the earnestness of their faith.

For me the question comes down to this: How was King David saved? David was far from perfect. He knew that he was a sinful man (see Psalm 51). But when he humbled himself, confessed his sin, and sought to follow God, God forgave him and went so far as to establish a special relationship with David and his descendants forever. If this could be true of David, isn't it possible that Jews today could so love, follow, and serve God that God would view them with favor on account of the Patriarchs, just as God did with David? There is no question in my mind that God would want Jews to know Jesus. But if they did not understand or accept the gospel, would such people who loved and followed God as David loved and followed God be rejected? Or is it possible that God would apply the merit of Christ to these people, who did not know or understand to ask for it?

The Jewish people are God's special covenant people. If they have yet to recognize Jesus as their Messiah, I believe that they will be judged according to the terms of the covenant they have known. Many Jews, as is true of many who claim to be Christians, may be turned away at the Last Judgment for failing to pursue God at all. But for those who have sought to love God with all their heart, soul, mind, and strength and have sought to love their neighbor as themselves, I believe the means by which God saved Abraham and Sarah, Moses and Zipporah, David and Bathsheba, is the same means by which God can save Jews today, while Christ's righteousness can be credited by God to their account.

A Challenge to Christians

There is one last word here for Christians about Judaism. Christians bear part of the responsibility—in fact, the greatest part—for the failure of the gospel among Jews. Christians have given their approval—sometimes directly, sometimes by their silence—to anti-Semitism. Not all Christians have done this, but far too many are guilty.

To be sure, Jews were oppressed before the advent of Christianity. But when Christianity became the official religion of the Roman Empire in 312, we offered theological support for such persecution. Since the church at that time became Roman, it stopped claiming that the Romans were the primary actors in killing Jesus. Instead, Christians claimed that the Jews crucified the Messiah—and since Jesus is divine in Christian theology, Christians went so far as to say that the Jews crucified God. Some still claim this. Christians began to preach that the Jews were a cursed people. Christians had taken their place as the "new Israel." The Jews were cut off from God. As recently as the late 1970s, the president of one of America's largest Protestant denominations publicly claimed that "God does not hear the prayer of the Jew."

The Crucifixion was not the doing of today's Jews, nor even of most of the Jews of Jesus' day. The accounts of the Crucifixion in the New Testament are meant to remind us that any of us might have been in that crowd shouting, "Crucify him!" It was the smallness of the human soul, the evil of a brutal empire, and the combined weight of the sin of the world that crucified Jesus on that day. Yet throughout the centuries Christians have laid the blame for the crucifixion of Jesus on the Jews—and in so doing have lent their tacit approval to the horrific crimes against Jesus' own people.

When I studied the persecution of Jews by the church, I read with shock the words of Martin Luther, the great Protestant reformer. In 1543, he wrote:

What shall we Christians do with this damned rejected race of Jews? First, their synagogues should be set on fire, secondly, their homes should likewise be broken down . . . thirdly, they should be deprived of their prayer books and Talmud.

Hundreds of thousands of Jews were put to death over the centuries, long before Hitler launched his "final solution." They were blamed for the Black Plague in Europe, and whole communities of Jews were murdered. They were segregated into ghettos. They were forced to convert to Christianity or leave countries like Spain. They were prevented from entering certain occupations. They actually were treated much better under Muslim authority during those centuries than under Christian rule.

This should make us weep, for surely it makes God weep. In fact, I believe it stirs the very wrath of God. The Bible that we read affirms that the Jews are God's people and that God wants us to bear witness of the love of Christ to them.

The Jews are God's covenant people. We Christians believe that, through faith, the grace of God, and the work of Christ, we also have become a part of God's covenant people. But how can we make such claims if we are not willing to build bridges and reach out with love to our Jewish brothers and sisters—not to convert, but simply to express the love of Christ and our gratitude for being a part of their extended family?

One of the most profound things I read regarding the sins of the Christian church toward Jews came from Pope John XXIII, who presided over Vatican II. Shortly before his death he wrote this prayer:

> We realize now that many, many centuries of blindness have dimmed our eyes, so that we no longer see the beauty of Thy Chosen People and no longer recognize in their faces the features of our first-born brother. We realize that our brows are branded with the mark of Cain. Centuries long has Abel lain in blood and tears, because we had forgotten Thy love. Forgive us the curse which we unjustly laid on the name of the Jews. Forgive us that, with our curse, we crucified Thee a second time.

I want to challenge you to hold our Jewish friends and neighbors in highest esteem. They are our older brothers and sisters in faith—first born. I want to encourage you to find points of commonality that you can celebrate and to rejoice in our shared love for God. Be bridge builders who bear witness to our faith with boldness, but also with great respect and reverence. I hope that you will encourage your Jewish friends to seek God, to call upon, know, and love God. I hope you will learn how, with respect and humility, to talk about your faith and the difference Christ has made in your lives. But I hope you also will listen and learn from your Jewish friends, because understanding their faith will do nothing but deepen your own.

CHAPTER 6

Christianity

For God so loved the world that he gave his only Son, so that everyone who believes in him may not perish but may have eternal life.

(John 3:16)

As we begin this chapter, I want to share with you why I undertook my own study of world religions. I pastor a church whose passion is reaching out to nonreligious and nominally religious people—thinking people who have serious questions about religion. When I speak with folks who are not involved in a church, they freely describe why they remain noncommittal when it comes to religion. They are generally interested in God, and they have spiritual questions. But they usually raise several objections to organized religion in general and to Christianity in particular, among which are questions about how Christians view other world religions.

Some of these people will say, "If there really is only one way, why are there so many different religions?" Others have said, "I am unwilling to make a commitment to Christianity when I have yet to study the other religions." Still others have told me that they believe all religions are saying basically the same thing and that they are equally valid paths to God. Many have told me that they find it inconceivable that God would condemn to hell those persons who were earnest God-seekers, who lived pious and just lives, and who sought to pursue God's will yet did not recognize Jesus Christ as God's Son. Such an assertion seems to them to be inconsistent with a God of love, mercy, and justice.

In this book I have sought to address, in a very simple way, each of these questions, objections, or concerns. I have attempted to offer a basic outline of how some of the major world religions began, a summary of the essential teachings of those religions, and a word about how they differ from and how they are similar to Christianity. I have suggested reasons why it is both illogical and dishonoring to the various religions to state that they are all essentially the same or that they are equally valid paths to God. I have maintained the traditional Christian view that Jesus Christ is God's only Son, the Savior and Lord, God's definitive Word, while at the same time raising the possibility that God's grace could be extended to those of other faiths who, in the words of Micah, seek to "do justice, and to love kindness, and to walk humbly with...God" (Micah 6:8). I have raised this possibility remembering that, according to the apostle Paul, it is only "by grace [we] have been saved through faith" (Ephesians 2:8) and that even this faith is a gift from God. I have suggested that God might look at the people of other religions and, based upon their faith, extend the salvation of Christ to them, even when they did not have the opportunity to know or receive Christ. If God does extend salvation to them, the day will come when "every knee [will] bend ... and every tongue ... confess that Jesus Christ is Lord" (Philippians 2:10-11).

Before this study was a book, it was a series of sermons I preached to my congregation. In each sermon we included videotaped interviews with the religious leaders of the various faiths we studied. (These sermons, upon which this book is based, can be ordered from my congregation's website at www.cor.org if you would like to hear them yourself, and two of them are included on the audio CD that comes with the hardbound version of this book.) In preparation for these sermons, and for the writing of this book, I read some of the sacred texts of each religion. I spent time, one on one, with the leaders of each of these faiths in my own city, listening to their faith stories. I attended worship services in each of these religions. I earnestly tried to understand and appreciate the message each proclaimed. Some in our congregation were at first a bit threatened by my willingness to preach on each of these faiths. Several asked, "Aren't you concerned that persons might listen to your sermons on the various religions and choose to leave Christianity?" My response was simple: "If Christianity is the truth, then we have nothing to be afraid of in studying other faiths. Doing so will only strengthen our faith and help us better understand what we believe."

By the end of my study, and at the conclusion of the sermon series, I had a deeper appreciation for the other religions. I found myself inspired and challenged by their teachings and practices. I saw numerous points of contact among the faiths, where our teachings paralleled one another. I also came to see fundamental and irreconcilable differences among the religions. But this study, far from weakening my faith, left me with even stronger convictions about the truth and power of the Christian gospel. While I became convinced that God's mercy toward people of other faiths must be broader than Christians often suppose, I also found I had a deeper longing to share the gospel with people of other religions, persuaded now, more than ever, that only in Jesus Christ do we find the definitive answer to the deepest longings of the human soul and the clearest revelation of God's character, his word for humanity, and his will for our lives.

I wrote this book with several goals in mind. For those of you reading this book who are undecided about your own faith, I hoped that this book would move you to consider pursuing the Christian faith and to become involved in a church. For those reading this book who are already people of faith, I hoped to help you think about other religions and to learn about them and from them, believing that you would discover that this study would actually strengthen your faith rather than weaken it. And finally, I hoped to help equip you who are Christians to be able to talk about your faith with persons of the other religions in a way that demonstrates respect, under-standing, and appreciation for them, while helping them hear the claims of the Christian faith in ways that are compelling. I felt this was an important goal of this book, recognizing that at times we Christians share our faith in ways that repel people from Christ instead of drawing them toward him.

In this I was reminded of Mahatma Gandhi's wonderful transformation of India and how it was prompted in part by his reading of the Sermon on the Mount, particularly the passages about how we respond to our enemies. Gandhi's nonviolence came right out of Jesus' teachings. Yet he was reported to have said, "I might have become a Christian but for the Christians that I have known."

I believe that Christians, in addition to learning how to bear witness to our faith more effectively, must learn to model for the world how people of faith can hold strong convictions while treating those of other religions with respect and humility, demonstrating a willingness to learn from them without compromising our own faith. Unless we can do this, I believe there is little hope for our world to move beyond the current armed conflicts among people of different faiths.

Now that we have considered other faiths, in this final chapter I would like for us to explore together some of the fundamental beliefs of the Christian faith as I understand them. As was the case with the other faiths, we will only scratch the surface of what Christians believe and why. In the end I will give my answer to the question, "Why Christianity?"

Let's begin our study of the Christian faith with what has been described as the simplest summary of the gospel, a passage of Scripture that even many who have never opened a Bible will recognize: John 3:16.

What Christians Believe

More Christians have memorized John 3:16 than perhaps any other verse in the Bible. It has been called "the gospel in miniature." It reads, "For God so loved the world that he gave his only Son, so that everyone who believes in him may not perish but may have eternal life." In this verse we find the essence of Christian theology. We find here a summary of the Christian view of the nature and character of God, of the human condition, and of the meaning and means of salvation. Let's briefly consider these points.

The Nature and Character of God

John 3:16 begins with an affirmation of the existence of God. The verse begins with God. Each of the major world religions has something to say about God. Let's consider these assertions for a moment.

For Buddhism, God is a nonessential idea: There may be a God; but if there is, God is uninvolved in our world. For Hinduism, God, or Brahman, is an impersonal force whose nature and will are only hinted at through the mythological stories of the multitude of gods. In Islam, God is the Almighty, the giver of the Quran, who demands adherence to this new word. In Judaism, God is the giver of the Law, seeking justice, righteousness, and obedience.

Christianity, in contrast, begins with a focus on the love of God. As 1 John 4:8 says, "God is love." Some of the other faiths affirm this idea, but for Christianity this is the starting point. God created human beings out of his desire to express love. We are created for fellowship with God. God's love motivates God to act. It is because God "so loved the world" that he acted in Jesus Christ. Everything else in the gospel springs forth from this idea.

The Human Condition

John 3:16, as a summary of the Christian gospel, notes that God acted to save humanity from perishing. Christianity sees the gospel as God's solution to a problem, and the problem is human sin and brokenness. Christianity takes an honest look at humanity and surmises that there is something wrong with us. Some believe Christians focus too much on sin. Perhaps some Christians do. But sin is not the dominant theme in Christianity.

Christians believe we are created in God's image and there is much good in us. We have the capacity to love people and to be selfless, kind, and just. Yet Christianity also notes that for all the good in us, evil is always close at hand. Christians make an honest assessment of the human condition. We believe the sinfulness of humanity cannot be ignored. Sin is the underlying cause of most of the pain, struggles, and tragedies in human existence. We all are born with this propensity to sin. As children, nobody taught us to lie or to think first of ourselves. It came naturally. Christians believe it is among the incontrovertible truths of the faith.

Each of the other faiths we have studied affirms that human beings sin. But none takes this idea so seriously as does Christianity. In fact, people of other faiths will note that this is a particular point on which we differ. So let's consider the point briefly.

The entire Hebrew Bible is the story of God's people and their failure to live up to God's covenants. Adam and Eve ate the forbidden fruit; Cain killed his brother Abel out of jealousy; the people of Babel wanted to build a tower so they could be gods; the people of Noah's day were perpetually violent. Even the heroes of the faith demonstrate this tendency to sin. Abraham lied about his wife to save his own neck. Moses killed a man. David committed adultery with Bathsheba. In the New Testament we read that Peter denied Jesus and that humankind crucified the Son of God.

In our own lives, we see this same tendency to sin manifested in myriad ways. We covet one another's possessions. We feel hate toward one another. We envy. We are self-absorbed, prideful, and prejudiced. Though we know the speed limit is fifty-five, we feel compelled to drive sixty. What in us makes it so hard to take criticism and yet so easy to hand it out? Why do nearly half of all marriages end in divorce? Why do we find it so easy to get caught up in materialism and so difficult to part with our money and possessions to serve God or to help those in need? Why does bigotry still rear its head? Why do we so easily tell "little white lies"? Why, despite our education and technology, can we not ensure that all human beings have access to adequate food, water supplies, and health care? Why as we enter the twenty-first century do we still resort to bloodshed in order to solve our conflicts? Human beings struggle with these things because our nature is marred by sin. It is part of our human condition.

Christianity not only recognizes our struggle with sin, it also makes plain that sin has consequences. Sin harms us, preventing us from experiencing the life God intends for us. Our sin harms others. Our sin separates us from God. On a broader scale, sin leads to broken societies. It leads to war, crime, and environmental disasters. Ultimately, sin leads to death—spiritual, physical, and eternal.

Christians believe that this view of sin is implicit in John 3:16. This verse tells us that God loves us. It also tells us that humanity is perishing. And it tells us that God does not wish us to perish. Because God loves us so much, God saw our human condition and wanted to do something about it. That is an important part of the good news of the Christian faith.

God's Plan

Because of this love, God chose to intervene on our behalf, to set the world on the right course. God acted through an historical event to deliver us from our sin. In this way the gospel is something like a vaccine for the human condition.

Christians believe that God acts in human history, seeking to save and redeem humankind. First God called Abraham and said, in essence, "I want you and your descendants to be a light to the nations so that people will see my relationship with you, and they'll choose to follow me and live in my light and be blessed."

Several hundred years went by and God said, "Maybe if I told humankind exactly what I was expecting of them, if I laid out the law in clear detail and told them exactly what to do day after day, then they would follow the path that leads to me and away from sin and death." And so God called Moses and through him gave Israel the Ten Commandments and the rest of the Law. Give human beings a law, however, and we will always try to find some way to wiggle out of it.

God then sent prophets, who said, "Please follow God. God has a plan that leads to life. If you don't follow it, terrible consequences will result." But the people killed the prophets and failed to listen and learn, and so consequences came. God withheld his protection from Israel. The Jews had to go into exile.

This is how Christians read the Hebrew Bible. It is the story of God's repeated attempts to lead humanity to walk in his ways and to pursue his path. It is also the story of humanity continually turning away from God.

What did God do next?

Christians believe that God decided to address sin once and for all, preparing a kind of remedy that would transform the recipients from the inside out. God's plan was that this remedy would begin with a handful of people who would see it and understand it. They would then share it with others, who in turn would share it with still others until the whole human race might be healed from the ailment of human sin.

What was this spiritual remedy? In the answer to that question we find the crux of the Christian gospel.

God did not send another prophet or book. Rather, God chose to become one of us. The Divine entered into our humanity.

Hindus and adherents of a host of other religions have suggested that God might appear as a human being from time to time. But this is not what Christianity asserts. Christians believe that God actually *became* human. In the person of Jesus, God was born, weak and frail. In Jesus, God experienced the wounds and joys of childhood. In Jesus, God experienced what it is to pass through adolescence and to enter adulthood. He knew temptation, hard work, frustration, disappointment, love, friendship, and even betrayal. When God, in the person of Jesus, was crucified, he knew what it was like to feel alone, even separated from God. An important part of the Christian gospel is that God has walked in our shoes.

This is only one part of the good news of the Christian gospel, however. Christianity also teaches that God became flesh, not simply to understand us, but that we might understand God. God's desire was that in Jesus Christ we might come to know the heart and character of God. We know only a short period of Jesus' life in any detail: the three-year period of his public ministry. The accounts in the Gospels describe his life, his teachings, his faith, his power, and his character. When we read the Sermon on the Mount, we take these teachings as a true reflection of the heart of God. When we see Jesus devoting his ministry to working with "lost" people, we believe we are witnessing the passion of God. When Jesus heals the sick, we are seeing the love and power of God. When Jesus cares for children, when he touches the untouchables of his day, when he tells stories about good Samaritans and prodigal children, we are privileged to be seeing God's desire, God's will, and God's nature.

But this was not all. Jesus became victim to the evil plots of humans. He was beaten and abused, humiliated and tortured; and then he died—nails piercing his hands and feet, a crown of thorns upon his brow—in order to deliver humanity. Here he was demonstrating the brokenness of humanity by showing, amazingly and tragically, that when God walked among us in human flesh, the most righteous and most powerful failed to recognize him and instead sought his destruction.

Yet Christians also see Jesus' suffering and death as redemptive. That is, on the cross God was taking upon himself the weight of the world's sins and the punishment that we deserve. The New Testament descriptions of Jesus' death are steeped in the language of animal sacrifice. That was a central part of the Judaism of that time. Today there are interesting theological discussions taking place about the meaning of Jesus' death, and various views are being put forth about how his death atones for our sins. Some theologians have rejected this idea altogether. We are so far removed from a world in which people regularly offer animal sacrifices as a means of atonement for their sins that it is difficult, at times, for us to understand completely the idea of Jesus' death as an offering or sacrifice for the sins of the world. But there are moments when the power of his death for the sins of the world comes into clear focus for us.

I am reminded of a young man who had made terrible mistakes while away at college, hurting himself and others. He came home for Christmas break, and, for reasons even he did not completely understand, among the first things he did was to come to our church and enter the sanctuary, where he saw the cross and wrapped his arms around it. He felt at a deep level the power of Jesus' death for *him*.

I knew of a woman who had been drinking and driving when she hit another vehicle and killed a child. She ended up in prison. When released, she could not forgive herself. She kept punishing herself over and over for what she had done. It was not until she came to see the cross of Christ as the place where God himself had made atonement for her sin that she was able to find hope. For her the statement that Christ died for her held great meaning—it was salvation, redemption, and deliverance.

In my own life, when I sin, I look at the cross and I understand that the forgiveness that I ask from God came at a price. I remember the lofty words of Dietrich Bonhoeffer in the opening chapter of his book *The Cost of Discipleship*, where he reminds us that the cross points to the costliness of grace. Jesus suffered for the sins of the world. He demonstrated to humankind the penalty that we deserve. He showed the extent of God's love. He bore the curse of humanity. He fulfilled the requirements of justice on our behalf.

Of course, the Christian gospel does not end with the cross. Jesus died on Friday. On Sunday, he was raised from the dead. In Jesus' resurrection God not only proved Jesus' identity as Savior and Lord, he sought to make clear that death is not the end for humanity. He robbed death of its power over us. In Christ's resurrection God addressed the angst the Buddha felt, not by calling us to renounce our love of life, but by demonstrating that sickness and aging and death are not the end of our story. As Jesus said, "I am the resurrection and the life. Those who believe in me, even though they die, will live" (John 11:25). How else would the God of the universe take away the sting of death for us except to send his Son to endure death and then rise again to render it impotent? Thus in Jesus' resurrection we find the ultimate triumph of good over evil, of grace over sin, of God over Satan, of life over death. And this fills us with hope.

Our Response

The Christian gospel offers us fundamental truths about God, about ourselves, and about salvation. It also calls for a response from us. But what kind of response? When confronted with the good news of God's grace, a first-century jailer asked the apostle Paul, "What must I do to be saved?" (Acts 16:30). Let's consider the Christian response to this question in contrast to the answer the other religions give.

Each of the other religions we have discussed offers its own answers to the question of salvation. In Hinduism, salvation is found in learning, over lifetime after lifetime, and in perfecting oneself through one's own effort until one can be reunited with God, as a drop of water is united with the ocean. In Buddhism, salvation comes through meditation over thousands of lifetimes as one lets go of desire and finally one's soul is snuffed out. In Islam, one is to yield oneself wholly to God and to pray, fast, pursue a pilgrimage, study and affirm the Quran, and fully integrate Quranic law into one's life. Believers hope that if they do this, Allah will accept them. In Judaism, salvation is found in pursuing the law of Moses and the teachings of the Talmud as one seeks to do good deeds.

All these faiths thus place salvation on the shoulders of human beings, teaching that we can save ourselves by working harder, learning more, pursuing five pillars, and/or eliminating desire. Christianity, in contrast, says that we cannot save ourselves. Christians believe that God turned the idea of salvation through works on its head. God said, in effect, "You haven't done such a good job of saving yourselves. So let's try this way. *I* will save you. *I* will set you free from your sin. *I* will love you. *I* will give you my Spirit to strengthen and heal you. *I* will give you a church family with whom you can grow in faith. *I* will offer you salvation. Your response is to receive my gift. If you do, I hope that this gift will transform your life and from this day forward you will live your life in grateful response to my salvation."

The Christian gains salvation only by God's grace. Salvation is a gift. All we can do is accept it. We believe. We trust. And we give thanks. The work was already done for us. We accept salvation as a gift, we trust in God, and then we live our lives in grateful response, not trying to earn something already given, but seeking to respond with love.

Some years ago a member of my congregation gave me a priceless gift—something for which he had sacrificed. When he started to hand me this gift and I saw how precious it was, I said, "I can't accept this. I'm sorry, but I simply cannot accept this gift you're giving me." His face became downcast; and he said, "Adam, I picked this gift out for you. I wanted you to have this. It is an expression of my love and gratitude for your ministry with me at a time of need."

How would you respond in such a situation—to a gift that was precious, a gift that you did not deserve? Some would insist on rejecting this gift, feeling that they were unworthy. Some would get out their billfold and say, "Well, OK, I'll take your priceless gift; but here, let me pay you for it. Here's twenty dollars." You know, intuitively, that such a response would be an insult! Twenty dollars for a priceless gift? A third possible response would be to accept this gift graciously and with humility and to understand it for what it is—an expression of love and care—and to live differently in response to this gift. It is this last response that God calls for us to make to his offer of salvation.

I believe God hopes that we will trust in him and in the sufficiency of Jesus Christ's work for us. I believe God hopes that we will invite him to apply the mercy of Christ to our lives. I am certain he wants us to seek to honor, love, and serve him with all that is in our lives, not in order to win our salvation, but in response to a salvation already given.

Christianity Through the Lens of the Other Religions

I hope that this study of world religions has helped you grow in your faith as a Christian. You may have found, as I did, unexpectedly, when I studied other religions, that each actually pointed me toward Christ. Here are some of the things I learned from the study.

Hinduism

Hinduism and its view of the unknowable God stood in stark contrast to the God of the Bible, who longs to be known. The sense that most Hindus may not have an intimate relationship with God made me appreciate the relationship with God Christianity offers through Christ. Yet the doctrine of karma in Hinduism had a great impact on me. Hindus believe that karma—one's good and bad deeds—carries forward not only in this life but also through cycle after cycle of reincarnations. This doctrine gave me a new way of speaking about the work of Christ. Jesus, the only perfect human being, offered his good karma—his righteousness—as a gift to humankind. Likewise, he suffered and died on the cross, taking upon himself the bad karma of the world.

Buddhism

Buddhism reminded me of the existential dilemma we all face. The Buddha's great concern was with the transience of all things, the fact that all of us will get sick, grow old, and die. He was right. His answer was to extinguish desire for health and life, so that one day, after thousands of lives, when all desire was finally suppressed, one could hope to be extinguished. But studying this faith gave me a deep appreciation for the Christian gospel. We do not seek to extinguish desire but to redirect it toward God's will. We embrace life and our relationships with others as good gifts from God. We find deliverance from our angst through the work of the Holy Spirit who comforts us and through the promise that God redeems our suffering and uses it for good. And we find peace and joy in the face of aging and death as a result of the hope of resurrection and eternal life with God.

Islam

Islam's emphasis on God's message to Mohammad reminded me of how grateful I am for something that Christianity affirms: When God sought to deliver a final, definitive word, it was not delivered through an angel speaking to a fallible human being. God did not depend on a person who, like us, would hear this word through his own sociological, cultural, and psychological filters. Instead, God became human—the Word became flesh—so that we might know God. When I read the Quran, which in places reads like the Hebrew Bible, I was grateful for the very different picture of God that Jesus painted for us—a God who calls us to love our enemies and to lay down our lives for others.

Judaism

Finally, in studying Judaism and the Law, the prophets, and the wide array of historical understandings of God found in the Hebrew Bible, I was more convinced than ever that Jesus is the Messiah of God, the fulfillment of the promises to Abraham, Moses, and David. No one else could have fulfilled these ideas as Jesus has. I love the Hebrew Bible; but, to me, the picture of God, and of God's saving work on behalf of humanity, is incomplete without the New Testament.

Why I Am a Christian

As we near the end of this book, I want to offer a statement of my own faith in the hope that it might help you articulate your own faith. There are many reasons why I am a Christian. I will include just six of them.

The Accounts of Eyewitnesses

I am a Christian because I believe the accounts of the eyewitnesses regarding Jesus' life, death, and resurrection. The apostles lived with Jesus for three years. They heard what he taught. They witnessed the miracles of healing he performed. They were there when he was arrested. They watched as he died. They were witnesses to his resurrection. And they passed down what they witnessed, first orally and then in written form. Though Luke was not an eyewitness, he interviewed many who were. Though Paul was not an eyewitness, he met Jesus on the road to Damascus in a way that turned his faith and his life in a completely different direction. I find the testimony of all these witnesses to be credible, and their credibility is enhanced by the ways in which involvement with Jesus after his resurrection so radically changed their lives.

The Christian Ethic

I am a Christian because I believe Christianity offers the most complete and authentically human way to live. Following Christ moves us to love our neighbors and our enemies. It challenges us to sacrifice something of ourselves for other people. It calls us to live a life of love.

Throughout the last two thousand years, many of the great social movements toward compassion for others sprang from the followers of Jesus. Underlying the civil rights movement in our own country, the end of apartheid in South Africa, and the movements to end slavery around the world are the teachings of Jesus. Christians started a large number of the schools and hospitals in the United States, as well as missions and social service agencies in our cities and communities. These good works have been undertaken by Christians because of the impact Jesus Christ has had on their lives and on the lives of so many others. Jesus said that his followers would be known by their love for one another, a love that is a reflection of God's love for us. This is part of the reason I am a Christian.

A Compelling Picture of God

I am a Christian in part because the picture of God painted by Jesus is, to me, the most compelling picture of God offered by any of the major religions. When Jesus looked on the multitudes as sheep without a shepherd and had compassion on them, I see a compelling picture of God. When Jesus chastised religious hypocrites but forgave a woman caught in adultery, I see a compelling picture of God. When he spent his time telling stories of the Kingdom to sinners who might not even have realized they were lost, I see a compelling picture of God. When Jesus calmed the storm on the Sea of Galilee, I see a compelling picture of God.

When Jesus opened the eyes of Bartimaeus, who cried out, "Jesus, son of David, have mercy on me!" (Mark 10:47), I see a compelling picture of God. When Jesus healed a man who wandered among the tombs, filled with demons, completely uncontrollable, I see a compelling picture of God. When Jesus met a woman at a well who had been divorced five times, and he offered her living water so that she would never be thirsty again, and then he made her an evangelist to her fellow Samaritans, I see a compelling picture of God.

On the last night of his life, when Jesus washed his disciples' feet in the manner of a slave, I see a compelling picture of God. When Jesus hung suffering on the cross, laying down his life for others, I see a compelling picture of God. And when God raised Jesus from the grave, having triumphed over evil and death and sin, I see a compelling picture of God.

I am a Christian because in Jesus I find the most authentic, moving, compelling picture of God and his love that I can imagine.

The Redemptive Power of the Cross

I am a Christian because of the redemptive power given us through Christ. He offers forgiveness—not cheap acceptance, but costly grace. Upon receiving that grace, people are changed; and a new life begins.

I have experienced that power in my own life. As a fourteen-year-old boy, I was lost. I was doing all the things that many kids do at that age. Then someone invited me to church, and they told me about Jesus. I gave my life to him, and I felt clean and new. God began to change me from the inside out, and I received God's unconditional love through Jesus in a way that I had never before experienced. The way I looked at the world began to change, as did the way I felt about myself. I am a Christian because of the gospel and its power to give new life to people whose lives have been spoiled by sin and brokenness.

Life After Death

I am a Christian because of the hope we have through Christ's resurrection from the grave and the promises of the Bible regarding our own life after death. When I minister to people at times of death, when I face the loss of people I love, when I contemplate my own mortality, I find in Christianity the peace and hope to live with joy.

As a pastor, I have performed hundreds of funerals. I do not know what I would say at those funerals were it not for the hope that Christianity offers. One Sunday morning, after our eight o'clock service, a member of our church came up and wrapped his arms around my neck and said, "I am so grateful for our church family and for the gospel of Jesus." His two-year-old granddaughter had died that week, and there was hope in Christ that he could not have found anywhere else. Recently I shared Holy Communion with a woman who had lost her husband a few weeks before. I knew this was a difficult weekend of worship for her. But she noted that being in worship reminded her of the hope she had to be reunited with her husband in Christ's eternal kingdom.

The Experience of Christ

Finally, I am a Christian because I have felt Christ's presence in my life. I have known what it is to be lost and then found. The most profound experiences of my life—the moments I have felt the greatest contentment, love, hope, and joy—all relate to my faith.

I have experienced a joy in prayer and praise and worship and mission that I have never experienced anywhere else. I experience a peace in my life with God that I cannot get by taking a pill or buying the latest toy at the electronics store. It is a peace that surpasses all understanding.

I am a better husband because I am a follower of Jesus. I am a better father and a better person because of what God has done daily in my life. The richest parts of my life come in relationship to God.

My personal experience of Christ is the reason I desire so

deeply for others to be his followers. My motive for reaching out and evangelizing in the name of Christ is not based on the fear that others might go to hell; rather, it emerges when I think of what others are missing in this life. Jesus Christ *is* life. If you do not know Christ, you are bypassing the best part of life. You are missing out on a peace and a joy whose equal you simply cannot find anywhere else. Jesus Christ has the capacity to make you into the person God intends for you to be. Jesus Christ gives you a purpose. His Spirit guides you. You have not really known life in its fullness until you have accepted him.

An Invitation

Jesus spoke of heaven as though it were a party, like a great wedding banquet, to which God sends out invitations to all. Some reject the invitations. Some are not interested in what he offers. Some reply that they are too busy at the moment to respond. We can refuse his invitation, of course. But when we do, we reject the gift he longs to give us; and we miss out on life—real life—life here and now and life eternal.

I will close this book by offering two simple prayers you might wish to pray.

If you are not a follower of Jesus Christ but would like to become one, you might take a moment to offer the first prayer, speaking these words out loud. If you are able, you may even want to kneel next to your bedside or bow where you are as you speak these words:

Jesus Christ, I would like to be one of your followers. Help me to do this. I accept the gift of salvation you offer. I put my trust in you. Help me to know you, to love you, to honor you, and to live for you. Forgive my sins. Wash me clean and make me new, as I commit my life to you. I receive you as my Savior and Lord. Amen.

This simple prayer is the first step in your Christian life. God has heard your prayer, and he loves you. Take the next step, and begin looking for a church in your community, talking with the pastor or another Christian friend about the decision you have made.

If you are already a Christian, I invite you to pray the second prayer:

O God, I continue to be grateful for the salvation you have offered me. I yield all that I am and all that I have to you. Help me to know, to love, and to follow you. Fill me with your Spirit, and draw me near to you. Grant me wisdom to understand your ways. Help me to love you with all that is within me. Help me to love my neighbor as I love myself. I recommit my life to you this day. Lord, help me to represent you well to those who do not know you. Help me to listen to, to learn from, and to love them. Help me to share my faith, first through my actions and then through my words. All of this I pray in Jesus' name. Amen.

My desire in writing this book was that God would answer your prayer, that you would find your own faith strengthened as a result of this study, and that others would see Christ through you. May God continue to lead you as you seek to know the One who is "the way, and the truth, and the life."

If you enjoyed this book, you may also enjoy:

**Christianity and World Religions:
Wrestling With Questions People Ask**

A Video-Based Small-Group Study
by Adam Hamilton

Study kit includes:
• *Christianity and World Religions: Wrestling With Questions People Ask*, Adam Hamilton's informative, thought-provoking book (multiple copies available)
• Videocassette and DVD containing six 15-minute presentations by Adam Hamilton—one per week for this six-week study—based on the six book chapters
• Leader's Guide with complete instructions for planning and leading weekly group sessions, including Scripture, discussion questions, leader helps, and activities for class sessions and home use
• Pastor's Guide with outreach tools on CD-ROM provides ways for expanding the small-group study into a churchwide and communitywide event
• Full-color vinyl case for display and storage

For more information, please go to www.abingdonpress.com.

CPSIA information can be obtained at www.ICGtesting.com
Printed in the USA
LVOW07s2351170616

493107LV00001BA/1/P